Living as Partners with God

Gila Gevirtz

EDITORIAL COMMITTEE
Chairman: Rabbi Jules Harlow

Rabbi Bradley Shavit Artson
Rabbi Morrison D. Bial
Rabbi Eugene B. Borowitz
Rabbi Nina Beth Cardin

Rabbi William Cutter
Dr. Barry W. Holtz
Rabbi Joy Levitt
Rabbi David Wolpe

BEHRMAN HOUSE, INC.

··◆··

DEDICATION

To Stephanie, Fred, Rami, Ilan, and Harry

May your lives be long and filled
with the joys of partnership, community, and Torah.

··◆··

ACKNOWLEDGEMENTS

With deep appreciation and affection for Ruby Strauss, my partner in creating this book.

Special thanks to the rabbis, educators, parents, and children
who generously contributed
to the development of Living as Partners with God.

PROJECT EDITOR: Ruby G. Strauss

BOOK AND COVER DESIGN: Pronto Design & Production, Inc.

ARTISTS: Joni Levy Liberman, Melanie Hall

PHOTO CREDITS: COVER: J.Grandy/SUPERSTOCK; THE STOCK MARKET: 8 Lightscapes, 22 Ron Sanford, 23 Mug Shots, 58 Craig Hammel, 60 Ed Bock, 74 P. Barton, 80 Larry C. Price, 84 Phillip Wallick, 85 Chris Hones, 92 Craig Tuttle, 110 Mug Shots, 113 Ariel Skelley, 122 Mug Shots, 124 Mug Shots, 128 Ron Lowery; CREATIVE IMAGE PHOTOGRAPHY: 10, 33, 38, 42, 50, 81, 97, 102, 106, 115; ILENE PERLMAN: 12; SUPERSTOCK: 16 P.Amranand, 45 Superstock; PALPHOT, LTD. Digital retouching: Demark Keller & Gardner Inc.: 26; SUNNY YELLEN: 32, 40, 95, 100; GILA GEVIRTZ: 34, 35; AMY AND ROBERT GEWIRTZ 64; FPG INTERNATIONAL: 78 T. Tracy, 120 A. Montes de Olo, 128 P. Gridley; UNITED FEDERATION OF METROWEST: 90; COMSTOCK: 96; FRANCENE KEERY: 103; RABBI NORMAN PATZ: 116.

Published by Behrman House, Inc.
Springfield, New Jersey 07081
www.behrmanhouse.com

ISBN 0-87441-614-0

Printed in U.S.A.

Contents

INTRODUCTION

Nation shall not lift up sword against nation,
neither shall they learn war anymore.

Isaiah 2:4

The Jewish people are dreamers of a most extraordinary dream. It is the dream of a complete and perfect world in which there is no hunger, war, or hatred—a world in which God's commandments are fulfilled and all God's creatures live in peace.

Passed on from generation to generation—from Abraham and Sarah to Moses, to Joshua, Deborah, and Hannah, to David and Solomon, to Elijah and Isaiah, to Judah Maccabee and Rabbi Akiba, and to their descendants—this dream has now been handed down to you.

But what good are hopes and dreams without a plan to make them real?

Our sages tell us that the very purpose of the Jewish people is to learn to live as a holy community so we can make our dream of a complete and perfect world come true. We believe that, together, we can succeed by living as partners with God.

As you read this book, you will see how each generation does its part and shares its experience and wisdom with the next. You will learn how to participate in the holiness of community and in the agreement, or Covenant, our people made with God thousands of years ago. And you will discover God's "voice" in Jewish history and in our holy texts.

You will also discover answers to many of your questions, questions such as, "What does it mean to be holy?" "How did the Jewish people come to have a dream?" and "What part can young people play in making our dream come true?"

We shall now meet many of the dreamers and heroes among our people. They will teach us how to live as partners with God. Let us share our questions and the answers we find as we discover ways to add holiness to our lives and honor our Covenant with God.

PART ONE

Understanding Our Covenant with God

It was not with our ancestors alone that Adonai made this Covenant, but with us, the living, every one of us who is here today.

Deuteronomy 5:2-3

On Passover, we open the door to invite the prophet Elijah to join our *seder*. Although we hope Elijah will announce that our dream of a complete and perfect world has come true, we know this has not yet happened. We know that God's commandments are not yet completely fulfilled and that God's creatures do not all live in peace.

However, we continue to be hopeful, for Judaism teaches that God delivered us from slavery in Egypt so we could live as partners with God and make our dream come true.

Why do you think we needed to become a free people to live as partners with God?

Following God's Ways

Every year at the Passover seder, Jews around the world read the Haggadah, the story of how we were delivered from slavery more than 3,500 years ago. We eat bitter herbs and greens dipped in salt water to remind us of the pain we suffered and the tears we wept when we were slaves in ancient Egypt. We recline comfortably in our chairs, thankful that we are now a free people, free to follow God's ways and help make the dream of a just and peaceful world come true.

OUR ANCESTORS WERE SLAVES IN EGYPT

Long ago, when our people were called the Children of Israel, or Israelites, they lived in Egypt and were enslaved by Egypt's ruler, Pharaoh. The Bible tells their story.

Pharaoh set cruel taskmasters over our people, masters who beat them and demanded they work from morning until night. But no matter how hard they worked, each day they were forced to work longer and harder than the day before.

Finally, our ancestors cried out. God heard their cry and commanded Moses to tell the Children of Israel, "God has seen your suffering and will free you."

Then God told Moses to go to Pharaoh and say, "Let My people go, that they may serve Me."

But Pharaoh would not let the Children of Israel leave. The Torah tells us, God sent ten plagues upon the Egyptian people. Overwhelmed by this punishment, Pharaoh permitted the Children of Israel to go.

As we read the names of the plagues at the Passover *seder*, we spill ten drops of wine. Some people do this by dipping a finger into the wine and then letting the drops fall onto a plate.

In the Book of Exodus we read that God sent Moses to Pharaoh to deliver this message: "Let My people go, that they may serve Me."

The words "Let My people go," are well-known. Although the words in the second half of the verse may be less familiar, they are as important. They teach us why God wants us to be free.

How can we serve God? How can we remind ourselves that the purpose of our freedom is to serve God?

THE PATH TO FREEDOM

The Israelites quickly gathered their belongings and followed Moses out of Egypt. But no sooner did they leave when Pharaoh had a change of heart and commanded his officers to bring them back.

Encamped near the Sea of Reeds, the Israelites were terrified by the unexpected sight of the Egyptian chariots pursuing them.

The Torah tells us that God then sent a strong wind from the east and split the Sea of Reeds in two. A dry path formed across the bottom of the sea and on each side there stood a wall of water. Quickly, the Israelites moved across the dry path.

Pharaoh's officers tried to follow but, as suddenly as the sea had parted, the walls of water came together, drowning the Egyptians.

Moses and the Children of Israel sang a song of praise to God for protecting them: "Who is like You among the gods, Adonai? Who is like You, majestic in holiness, awesome in splendor, doing wonders?" And Miriam, the sister of Moses, played the timbrel as she led the women in a dance of celebration.

Our tradition teaches that God cleared the path for the Israelites as they crossed the sea. With a mighty hand and an outstretched arm, God brought our people to safety and freedom.

Our sages tell us that when the Egyptians were drowning in the Sea of Reeds, the angels celebrated and sang. God silenced them, saying, "How can you sing while My creatures are drowning?"

What do you think the sages wanted to teach us?

HEBREW LESSON

Holy

קָדוֹשׁ

God freed the Israelites from slavery so they could make the Covenant, or agreement with God, and become a holy people, an *am kadosh*. The word *kadosh*, "holy," describes God's path. When we follow God's commandments by praying, studying Torah, and fulfilling other *mitzvot*, we follow God's holy ways and we live as partners with God.

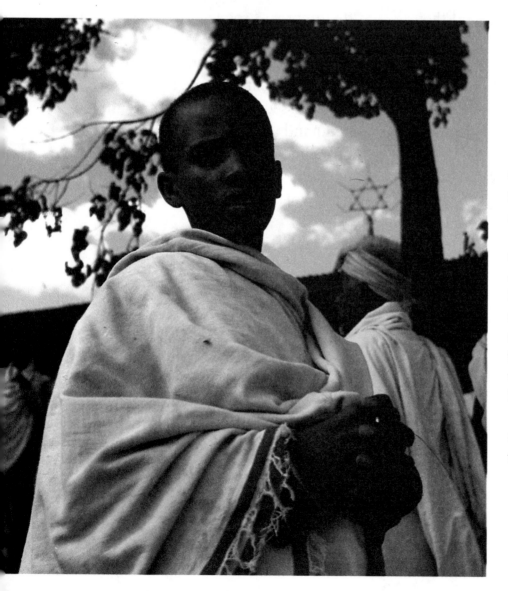

God freed the Israelites from slavery in Egypt. Almost 4,000 years later, in 1985, the Jewish communities of Israel and North America saved the Jews of Ethiopia from oppression and famine in a dramatic airlift that brought them to freedom in Israel. The airlift was called "Operation Moses."

Why do you think the rescue mission was given this name?

THE LESSON OF THE EXODUS

Every year we retell the story of our Exodus from Egypt. It teaches an important lesson: although all people were created in God's image—*b'tzelem Elohim*—we can follow God's ways only when we are free to serve God.

As God heard the cries of the Israelites, so we can pay attention to the needs of people around us. As God delivered the Children of Israel from slavery, so we can help people who are oppressed.

God provides rain to water crops and quench the thirst of all living things. How can you follow God's ways when you see a wilted plant or a thirsty pet? God provides loving friends and family to cheer us when we are sad or ill. How can you follow God's ways when someone you know is unhappy or sick?

Every day is filled with opportunities to be kind and considerate, helpful and caring. When we use these opportunities, we live as partners with God.

The Bible tells us to "Serve God with a whole heart and a willing mind." Do you think it's possible to serve God well if your efforts are "half-hearted" or your mind isn't willing? Why?

Do you think it's possible to become enslaved by something other than a person? For example, how might jealousy, greed, or anger control your behavior? How might prayer help free you from such enslavement? What else could help free you?

Three Wishes

We celebrate Passover as if we ourselves had been slaves in Egypt and were personally freed from that harsh life. We eat *maror* at the *seder* to remember the bitterness of slavery. We eat *matzah* to remind ourselves of our quick departure from Egypt. And we recline on pillows as a sign of the freedom we enjoy today.

As a slave in Egypt, what three things do you think you would have wished for? Why?

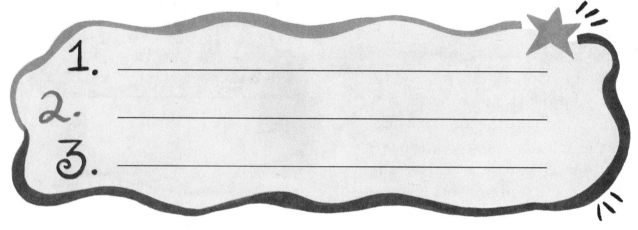

1. _____

2. _____

3. _____

A Song of Praise

Moses and the Children of Israel sang a song praising God for delivering them from slavery to freedom.

Write a song that expresses your joy in being free to live a Jewish life. As you write the words on the lines below, think about the music. You can make up your own or use the melody of a song you already know.

Do You Know How It Feels?

In the Book of Exodus, we are told not to mistreat a stranger, "for you know how a stranger feels, having yourselves been strangers in the Land of Egypt." Yet sometimes people are unkind or even cruel to outsiders, people who look or behave differently than they do.

Have you ever felt like an outsider? Perhaps you moved to a new neighborhood or started going to a new school, or were dressed a bit differently than your classmates. List three words that describe how you felt:

What could someone have done to help you feel better?

When you see a classmate being treated as an outsider, how can remembering what it feels like help you show kindness?

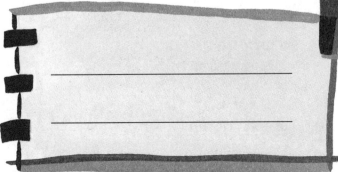

How can knowing that kindness and compassion are God's ways remind you to treat others fairly?

15

Each spring, caterpillars change into butterflies, seeds sprout and blossom into flowers, and silent tadpoles turn into croaking frogs. How do the changes brought by the seasons help you feel God's presence?

Have you ever wished that, like nature, you could help turn the world into a more beautiful and friendly place? If you could do one thing to make a better world, what would it be? How might you do it?

2

Sharing God's Holiness

Jewish tradition teaches that God's holy presence can be found in the wonders of our daily life—in the tiny, perfect hand of a newborn baby, and in the grace and power of an eagle in flight.

Why do the natural wonders of the world still seem amazing even when you understand the scientific explanations for them? What daily wonders of your own growth remind you that God is present?

From ancient times, the Jewish people have believed that God's presence fills the world. When we pay attention and follow God's holy ways, we live as partners with God and help complete the world. These beliefs gave our people the courage to follow Moses out of Egypt and make a special agreement with God.

HEBREW LESSON

Brit
Covenant

בְּרִית

Brit is the agreement the Jewish people made to live in partnership with God. This Covenant also makes us partners with all the generations of our people who came before us. Because they kept the Covenant and passed the tradition on to us, we can continue to live as a holy people.

OUR COVENANT WITH GOD

Our tradition teaches that God delivered the Israelites from slavery so they would be free to make an agreement, or covenant, to live as partners with God. God promised to teach the Jewish people how to turn even the most ordinary moments into holy ones. God spoke to the people at Mount Sinai, saying, "If you obey My laws faithfully, you will be My treasured possession. You will be a holy nation."

The Israelites promised to keep the laws of the Covenant. They said, "all that God has spoken we will do."

When the Children of Israel made the Covenant with God, they made it for themselves, their children, their children's children, and all generations after them—then, now, and forever.

No one knows which mountain in the Sinai wilderness is Mount Sinai. The story is told that all the mountains wanted to be chosen. They called out to God, "Choose me, for I am the mightiest," "Choose me, for I am the tallest," "Choose me, for I am the oldest." Only one mountain stood in silence, too modest to speak before God. Because of its modesty, God chose it as the one on which to give the Torah to our people.

THE INSTRUCTIONS FOR LIVING AS A HOLY PEOPLE

The Torah tells us that after entering into the Covenant with the Israelites, God told Moses they were ready to receive the *mitzvot*, the commandments for living as a holy people.

Early in the morning on the appointed day, the sky suddenly turned black as pitch and the crash of thunder rumbled and roared across the sky. The Israelites stood in awe as bolts of lightning streaked the heavens with the sharpness of a knife, and the blast of a *shofar*, a ram's horn, grew louder and louder.

Then, as suddenly as the deafening sounds had come, they stopped. All was silent.

The Torah tells us that God spoke and the Israelites received the Ten Commandments.

After the Ten Commandments were given, Moses received the other laws of Torah from God. And Moses taught the *mitzvot* to the Children of Israel so they could become a holy people, an *am kadosh*.

The Ten Commandments
1 I am Adonai your God who brought you out of Egypt.
2 Do not have other gods beside Me or pray to idols.
3 Do not use My name except for holy purposes.
4 Remember Shabbat and keep it holy.

5 Honor your father and mother.
6 Do not murder.
7 Do not take another person's husband or wife.
8 Do not steal.
9 Do not swear falsely.
10 Do not desire what belongs to your neighbor.

What would it mean to live as a Jew if we had not received the *mitzvot*?

Living as Partners with God, We Help Complete the World

Each of us can share in God's holiness and help complete the
world by observing the *mitzvot*.

RODEF SHALOM (SEEKING PEACE)

The word *shalom* comes from the
same root as the Hebrew word
shalem, which means "whole" or
"complete." Judaism teaches that, as
partners with God, we must help
bring peace into the world and into
our families, for the world cannot be
complete without it.

TZEDAKAH

The word *tzedakah* comes from the
Hebrew word *tzedek*, which means
"justice." When we give *tzedakah* to
people in need, we add justice to
God's world. Did you know that all
of us, even those who are poor, are
commanded to give *tzedakah*? Why
do you think this is so?

SH'MIRAT HA-LASHON (GUARDING YOUR TONGUE)

The gift of speech is precious, for words have great power to hurt or to heal.
Understanding this, Judaism teaches us not to gossip. How can words of praise
for God help heal when your heart aches? How can words of apology help heal
when you've argued with a friend?

TEFILLAH (PRAYER)

The word *tefillah* comes from the same root as the Hebrew word meaning to "judge." Our tradition teaches that prayer helps us judge how well we are living as creatures made *b'tzelem Elohim*, in God's image.

When we pray, we praise God for the good in our lives and ask for the determination to become better people. How can *tefillah* bring you closer to God? How can it bring you closer to other people?

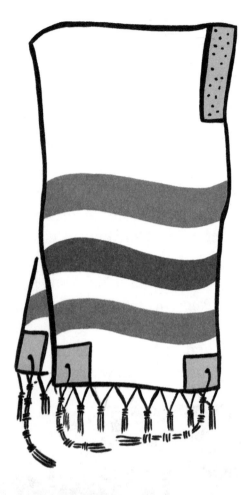

SH'MIRAT SHABBAT (SABBATH OBSERVANCE)

The Torah teaches that Shabbat is a sign of our Covenant with God. We honor Shabbat by resting and joining others in celebration and *tefillah*. What else can you do on Shabbat to help you enjoy the wonderful world God created?

The *Brit* is the Jewish people's Covenant to live in partnership with God. We honor this agreement by fulfilling *mitzvot*.

ONLY HUMAN BEINGS CAN PERFORM *MITZVOT*

All life is holy, but only human beings are given the ability to add to life's holiness through the *mitzvot*. For example, all animals need to eat, but only human beings can turn mealtime into holy time by reciting *Ha-Motzi*, the blessing over bread, and *Birkat Ha-Mazon*, the blessing after meals. Only human beings can make their homes into holy spaces through acts of hospitality, *hachnasat orḥim*. And only human beings can understand the importance of holidays, *ḥagim*, and add to their holiness through song and prayer.

Everything that brings us closer to God and helps us live as partners with God is *kadosh*. That is why prayers are holy; words of forgiveness are holy; acts of charity and the study of Torah are holy; and Shabbat and *ḥagim* are holy.

How can you treat your family so that you add to the love in your home? How can you celebrate Shabbat so that you add to the joy of your week? How else can you add to life's holiness and help complete the world?

A bear can fish for food, but it can't recite a blessing before eating. Only human beings have been given the ability to perform *mitzvot*. How can knowing this fact help when you have an urge to ignore an opportunity to recite *Ha-Motzi* or to perform other *mitzvot*?

The Torah teaches: "You shall not insult the deaf or place a stumbling block before the blind." Our sages explained that this means we should not take advantage of other people. How can your awareness of God's presence help you treat others with respect?

MITZVOT BEGIN WITH AN AWARENESS OF GOD

Our tradition teaches that when we live with an awareness of God's presence, we become alert to the opportunities to share in God's holiness by performing *mitzvot*.

How can an awareness of God's presence help you turn your treatment of others into holy acts? For example, how can it help you fulfill the *mitzvah* of kindness—*gemilut ḥassadim*, or visiting the sick—*bikkur ḥolim*?

To give *tzedakah* with an awareness of God's presence is to see a reflection of God in other people. To care for pets and plants with an awareness of God is to remember that all God's creations are holy.

When you live with an awareness of God's presence by fulfilling the *mitzvot*—honoring your parents, giving food to the hungry, observing Shabbat, reciting blessings, and caring for plants and animals—you work in partnership with God to complete the goodness of the world.

You are important, a member of our Covenant with God. And the *mitzvot* you fulfill help make the world a better place.

Torah Is Our Marriage Certificate

The partnership between God and the Jewish people is sometimes compared to a loving marriage. Our sages tell us that at Mount Sinai, God was the groom, the People of Israel the bride, and the Torah our marriage contract, or *ketubah*.

In the space below, copy the Ten Commandments on page 19 and decorate the border like a *ketubah*.

1

2

3

4

5

6

7

8

9

10

◆ ◆ ◆ ◆ ◆ ◆ ◆ ◆ ◆ ◆ ◆ ◆ ◆ ◆ ◆ ◆ ◆ ◆ ◆ ◆

Actions Speak Louder than Words

The Jewish people made a promise to keep God's laws. However, because we are human, we sometimes talk about the commandments we plan to observe but fail to take the actions.

What do you think the expression "actions speak louder than words" means?

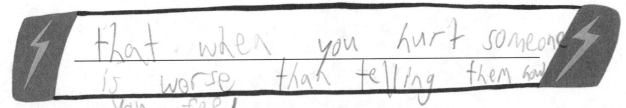

that when you hurt someone is worse than telling them how you feel

Write two actions that say, "We are keeping the Covenant between the Jewish people and God."

trust

a promise

A Sign of Agreement

When an agreement is made, there are sometimes special signs that become reminders of it. For example, a handshake is sometimes used as a sign that a business agreement has been made, and wedding bands are used as a sign that people are married. The Bible tells us that after the Flood, God made a *brit* with Noah not to bring another Great Flood. The rainbow became a sign of that covenant.

Imagine that you were to enter into a *brit* with your family to make your home a more peaceful place. What might you each agree to do?

Describe or draw a picture of the sign you might use to remind one another of your agreement.

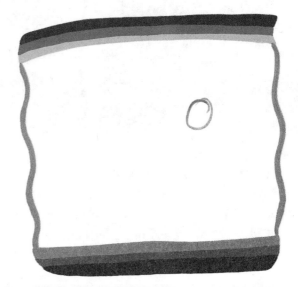

Jerusalem is the capital of the State of Israel. Did you know that King David lived in this city over 3,000 years ago? From ancient times when Jews gathered to pray in the Holy Temple built by King Solomon, to the hustle and bustle of today, the hills of Jerusalem have echoed with the words of Torah and the yearning of our people to live as partners with God.

In 1996, we celebrated the 3,000th birthday of the holy city of Jerusalem with prayer, song, and fireworks. What do you think makes the city holy? How can people add to its holiness?

God's Holy Land

Suppose your family attended synagogue services not only with the members of your congregation, but with all your Jewish friends and relatives: friends from camp and from music lessons; friends from scouts and sports; and aunts, uncles, and cousins from cities all over North America and other parts of the world.

Imagine that every Jew gathered in one place to pray. Where would be the best place for such a gathering? Why do you think so?

In ancient times, all Jews lived in the Land of Israel. Three times a year—on the festivals of Sukkot, Passover, and Shavuot—they made pilgrimages from their homes to pray in one place, the Holy Temple in Jerusalem.

An ancient legend explains how the location of the
Holy Temple, *Bet Ha-Mikdash*, was chosen.

The Field of Loving Kindness

Long ago, in the days of King Solomon, two brothers had a farm on
the outskirts of Jerusalem.

One brother had six children. The other had none. Year after year, the
brothers shared their harvest of wheat.

One autumn night, the younger brother lay in bed thinking, "My
brother has so many mouths to feed. It isn't fair that he receives only

half the harvest of our field." So he rose from his bed and took three bundles of wheat from his portion and placed them with his brother's.

That very night, the older brother tossed and turned in his bed. He thought, "My brother has no children to provide for him when he is old. It isn't fair that he receives only half the harvest." So he rose from his bed and took three bundles of his wheat and placed them with his brother's portion. In the morning both brothers were astounded to find their piles of wheat just as they had been the day before.

Every night of the harvest, each brought a portion of his wheat to the other. And each morning they found their piles of wheat remaining as they had been at nightfall.

Finally, one night the two brothers happened to meet in the middle of the field, each carrying wheat for the other. Understanding what had happened, they put down the bundles of wheat and embraced.

When the time came to build the *Bet Ha-Mikdash*, God led King Solomon to the field. "This is where you shall build My holy Temple. For the Temple must be built on a foundation of loving-kindness." And so the *Bet Ha-Mikdash* was built on the very spot where the brothers embraced.

Why do you think the legend tells us that God declared that the Holy Temple had to be built on a foundation of loving-kindness?

Our tradition teaches that we can make our homes into sanctuaries, or temples, by performing acts of loving-kindness. What can you do to make your home into a holy place?

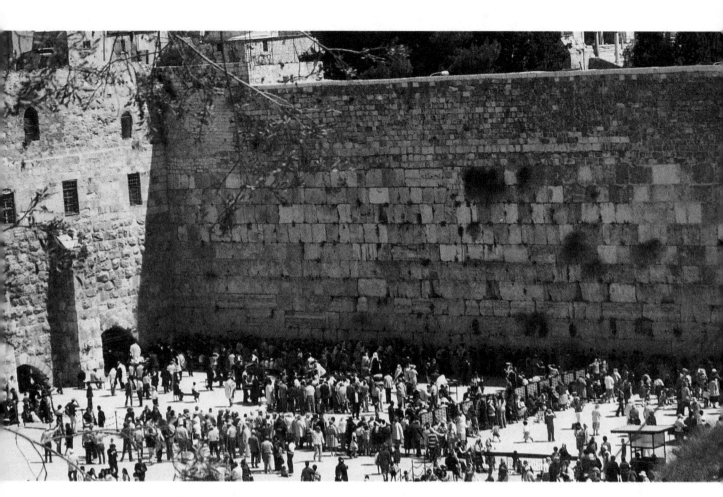

Part of the wall surrounding the Temple Mount still stands today. It is called the *Kotel*—the Western Wall. Thousands visit the *Kotel* each week. Why do you think Jews from all over the world come here to pray?

THE PROMISE OF THE HOLY LAND

The Torah teaches that God promised the Land of Canaan (which is what Israel was called long ago) to Abraham and Sarah—for their family and descendants. God's promise is repeated many times in the Torah, so Israel became known as the Promised Land.

The Torah also teaches that God fulfilled the promise by delivering our ancestors from slavery and bringing them to the place where we were first able to live according to God's commandments.

The Land of Israel, *Eretz Yisrael*, is the home of some of the holiest places and events in Jewish history. That is why we also call it our Holy Land.

The patriarchs—Abraham, Isaac, and Jacob—and the matriarchs—Sarah, Rebecca, Rachel, and Leah—lived in *Eretz Yisrael*. Deborah, Gideon, and Judith bravely defended

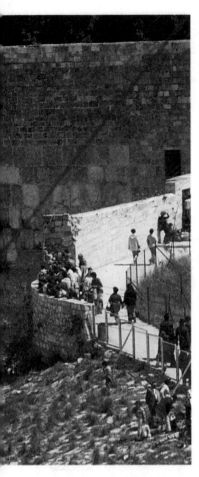

Israel against its enemies. King Saul, King David, and King Solomon reigned over Israel. And Jeremiah, Amos, and Isaiah were prophets in Israel.

The Temple where our ancestors prayed was built in the Land of Israel—in Jerusalem, the holiest city in the world for Jews. And Hebrew—the holy language of Torah—was spoken in *Eretz Yisrael*.

The Hebrew word *Yisrael* means "to struggle with God and succeed." *Yisrael*, the name of both our people and our holy land, reminds us that the Jewish tradition is one of struggle and courage. Our struggle is to live as an *am kadosh*. And throughout the generations our courage has come from God and the wisdom of Torah.

A Tradition of Courage and Struggle

When the Romans conquered the Land of Israel almost 2,000 years ago, the Jews were exiled. But they carried the Torah with them to the four corners of the earth. Each generation passed the teachings of the Torah and of our sages on to the next. And each generation prayed that *Eretz Yisrael* would one day be ours again so we could live as an *am kadosh,* a holy people, in our own land.

Through the centuries, there have been many other exiled peoples who have also been forced to leave their homelands. But in time each ceased to be a people, for without a country they had no reason to stay together. Jews are the only exiled nation that remained one people, even though we had to wait 2,000 years to return to our Holy Land.

We can enjoy a "taste" of Israel, without even being there. Have you ever eaten falafel and hummus on pita bread? Delicious!

THE MODERN STATE OF ISRAEL

It was not until almost 20 centuries had passed that *Eretz Yisrael*, the Land of Israel, became a Jewish State once more. The modern State of Israel, *Medinat Yisrael*, was born on May 14, 1948.

At long last, we had a state of our own—a place where Jews would always be welcome. Survivors of the Holocaust came from Germany and eastern European countries to begin new lives. Jews came from countries such as Yemen and Morocco where, for centuries, they had lived in poverty and danger. Others came from America and Canada to rebuild the Land.

Medinat Yisrael breathed new life into the Jewish people. It restored our pride and our strength as schools, libraries, synagogues, hospitals, and museums were built, and the desert was made to blossom.

Many Jews have moved to Israel, and each year more and more visit. Many families vacation there while others work or study in Israel for a year or six months.

IT'S A *MITZVAH* TO LOVE ISRAEL

From ancient times, the sages taught that it is a *mitzvah* to love the Land of Israel. This *mitzvah*, called *ahavat Tziyon*—love of Zion—is God's reminder that *Eretz Yisrael* was given to us as part of the Covenant and is a blessing for us all.

We show our love for Israel in many ways. We visit, plant trees to rebuild the land, and celebrate the State of Israel's Independence Day on Yom Ha'atzma'ut. We recite words of love for *Eretz Yisrael* in prayers such as the *Amidah* and *Birkat Ha-Mazon*—the Grace after Meals. And we share in our ancestors' love and devotion when we repeat the words of the prophet Isaiah, "Rejoice with Jerusalem and be glad for her!"

How do you think our faith in God and love of Torah helped keep alive our dream of returning to the Land of Israel? How do you think our love of Israel helps Jews around the world remain as one community?

These children are singing Israel's national anthem, *Hatikvah*, "The Hope." The words are, "As long as a Jewish heart beats and as long as Jewish eyes look toward the east, then our 2,000-year hope to be a free nation in the Land of Zion is not lost." Can you imagine what it's like to hope and dream about something for 2,000 years?

What do the words of *Hatikvah* tell you about the Jewish people's continuing love of Israel?

WHEN YOU'RE IN ISRAEL . . .

The colors of *Medinat Yisrael* aren't just the blue and white of its flag. They're the red of Haifa's wild poppies, the green of Ein Gedi's oasis, the orange of Jaffa's orchards, and the rainbow of colors that appear in daily life.

On a hot day nothing tastes as good as a glass of freshly squeezed carrot juice or a double scoop of chocolate chip *glidah* (ice cream).

The street signs are "user friendly." They're written in three languages: Hebrew, Arabic, and English.

While waiting at a bus stop you can practice your Hebrew. Can you find the word "ketchup"?

34

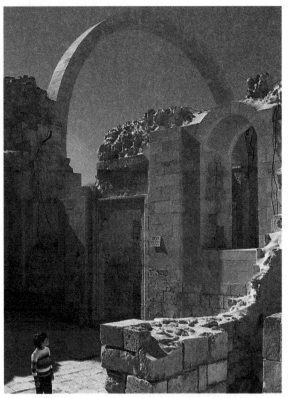

The shopping mall in Tel Aviv is like those in America, except that you can buy falafel at the snack bar and storekeepers wish you "Shabbat shalom" on Friday afternoon.

In *Eretz Yisrael*, you don't just read about our ancestors, you can stand where they stood and see what they saw.

Even Mickey Mouse is impressed by how the Israelis made the Negev desert bloom.

You might be tempted to ride home on a donkey like this one just as our ancestors did in biblical times.

For the Love of Israel

Judaism teaches us to remember our Holy Land by facing toward Jerusalem when we pray. In North America the Holy Ark is usually located on the eastern wall of the synagogue and we face it when praying. Inside this ark, list three ways you can show your love for the Land of Israel.

Making Dreams Come True

Our dream of a Jewish state has come true and we continue to hope and pray for peace in *Eretz Yisrael*.

Write a poem or prayer about your hope for *shalom* in *Eretz Yisrael*.

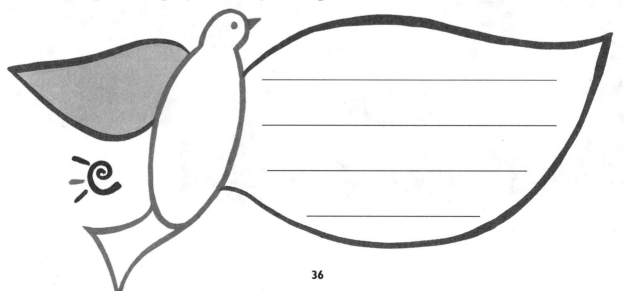

Visit Israel Now!

Create a travel poster for Israel. State at least one reason why people will enjoy visiting Israel and then illustrate the poster with a scene of Israel. For example, you might say, "Come Back to Your Homeland" and illustrate the poster with a picture of Tel Aviv, Jerusalem, or Beersheva.

Sarah is practicing the Torah portion she will read when she becomes a *bat mitzvah* next week. She has also learned the *haftarah*, the weekly portion from the prophets. Soon you will have the opportunity to become a *bar* or *bat mitzvah* and chant a *haftarah* for your congregation. Perhaps your portion will be from the Book of Isaiah, or from Jeremiah, or Ezekiel.

Every week of the year, whether or not there is a *bat* or *bar mitzvah* celebration, a *haftarah* is chanted as part of the Shabbat service in the synagogue. What does this tell you about the importance of the teachings of the prophets?

The Message of God's Prophets

Have you ever seen your friends do something you believed was wrong? Perhaps you saw them throw stones at a stray cat, or tease a classmate about his clothes, or take a candy bar without paying.

Did you tell your friends they had done something wrong and explain why, or were you afraid to speak up? How did you feel? What did you do?

Among the greatest teachers of the Jewish tradition are the ancient Israelite prophets. They were God's messengers to am Yisrael. Each one had the courage to speak up against wrong, and the wisdom to provide guidance. The writings of the prophets teach us how to live as a holy people.

Who Were God's Prophets?

The stories of the prophets are found in the 21 books that make up the section of the Bible called *Nevi'im*, Prophets.

Some prophets were wealthy; others were poor. Some lived in the Land of Israel; others in foreign lands. But the prophets all had one thing in common: They all brought God's message to the people. The prophet Nathan, for example, told King David he had sinned and would be punished.

Elijah spoke out against idol worship. And Jeremiah warned the people they would no longer be able to live in the Promised Land if they treated one another unfairly.

▲▲▲▲▲▲▲▲▲▲▲▲▲▲▲▲▲▲▲▲▲▲▲▲▲▲

The Bible *(Tanach)* is divided into three sections: *Torah* (The Five Books of Moses), *Nevi'im* (Prophets), and *Ketuvim* (Writings).

Which prophets can you name?

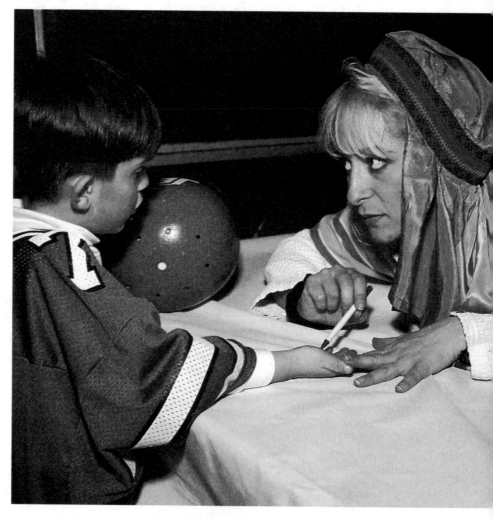

It can be fun to visit the fortune-teller's booth at a Purim carnival, but a fortune-teller's words are not meant to be taken seriously. No one can know your future before it happens.

The Israelite prophets were not fortune-tellers, and their job was not to entertain. They cared deeply about the Jewish people and the responsibility to fulfill our Covenant with God. For example, Isaiah said, "Share your food with the hungry."

Why do you think it might not be fun to hear the message of a prophet? Why do you think it would be important to listen to the message anyway?

THE PROPHET MICAH

Over 2,500 years ago, in the days of the prophet Micah, the Israelites lived in the Holy Land but many ignored our Covenant with God. They did not keep the promise to live as an *am kadosh*.

Disregarding the Second Commandment, they bowed down before idols. Forgetting that God demands justice, truth, and mercy, they ignored the needs of widows and orphans. The rich were selfish and oppressed the poor, and the rulers were dishonest. In time, injustice, greed, and cruelty spread like a plague throughout the Land.

Micah warned the Israelites that they would become weaker and weaker, and their lives more wretched, if they continued to stray from God's path. But seeing their suffering, Micah also brought God's message of hope. Micah taught that God will strengthen and renew us. He said, "Adonai requires only that you do justice, love mercy, and walk humbly in God's ways."

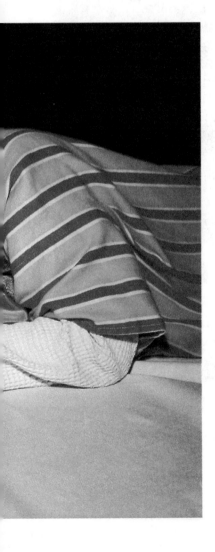

Why do you think our people still read and find hope in Micah's teachings?

What *mitzvot* can you fulfill to show your love of truth and kindness?

Why is giving *tzedakah* a good way to show your love of justice?

THE TEACHINGS OF GOD'S PROPHETS

Thousands of years have passed since the days of the prophets, but we continue to hear God's voice through their writings.

From the prophets Isaiah, Zechariah, and Hosea we learn that our observance of holidays and rituals are important but that fulfilling these *mitzvot* pleases God only if we also observe the *mitzvot* of treating each other with respect, kindness, and justice. Do you think it would make sense to fast on Yom Kippur but ignore those who are hungry all year long? Would it make sense to build a *sukkah* but forget about people who are homeless? How can fulfilling holiday *mitzvot* remind us to help care for others?

When the Israelites behaved in arrogant ways, thinking they were better than other peoples, God reminded them through prophets, such as Amos and Jonah, that all people are loved and valued equally by God. That is why God sent the prophet Jonah to the non-Israelite city of Nineveh to warn the people that

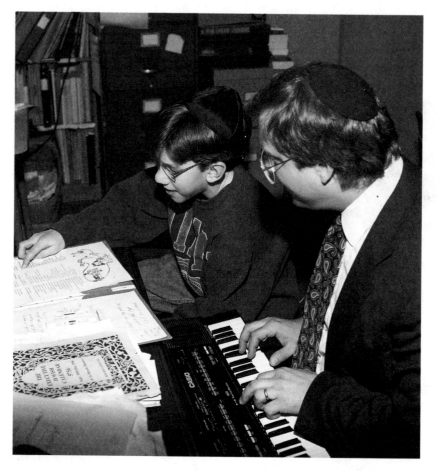

This cantor is using a keyboard to teach his student how to chant a *haftarah*, or weekly portion from *Nevi'im*. Why do you think we chant the portions from the Torah and Prophets rather than just reading the words?

they would be destroyed if they didn't repent the evil they had done.

The prophet Elijah taught that God did not create Jews differently from other people, but that because we promised to live as an *am kadosh*, there are times when we must behave differently than others. For example, when we see people fighting, we are instructed to help bring a peaceful resolution to the argument, fulfilling the *mitzvah* of being a *rodef shalom*.

LIVING THE LESSONS OF THE PROPHETS

In synagogues, schools, and homes throughout the world, generations of Jews have studied the teachings of the prophets. We continue to pass on their wisdom so that each new generation can be guided and strengthened.

When we perform *mitzvot*, we are like a lamp that lights the darkness so others can see the goodness of God's ways.

Think about it. How can the behavior of one person or group of people be a good influence on others? For example, if you speak respectfully to a competitor in a sports activity, might that person be influenced to be respectful too?

Suppose you were running against a classmate in a school election and you believed you were the best candidate. Would it be all right for you to lie or make fun of your opponent? Why or why not?

The prophets' message that God loves justice has given our people courage to protest acts of prejudice and hate. Their reminder that God is compassionate has inspired many Jews to dedicate their lives to helping others by becoming doctors, police officers, social workers, and teachers. And the prophets' call for goodness and mercy has taught us that it is not just nice, but our *duty* to give *tzedakah* often and generously.

Most of all, the prophets teach us that living a life of Torah—loving justice, showing kindness, and fulfilling God's *mitzvot*—is what is most important. For when we do, we share in God's holiness and become stronger.

HEBREW LESSON

Compassion and Mercy

רַחֲמָנוּת

God is often called *Ha-Raḥaman*, the Merciful One. Like a loving parent, God comforts us when we suffer and helps us become strong. How can you follow God's ways by showing mercy and compassion—*raḥamanut*—to others?

Lessons from the Prophets

Let not the wise glory in their wisdom, nor the strong in their strength, nor the rich in their riches. But let them glory in their understanding and knowledge of God.

Jeremiah 9:22-23

Did not one God create us? How then can we be dishonest and hurtful to one another if we are sisters and brothers?

Malachi 2:10

Speak the truth, judge others honestly and peacefully, and do not make plans to harm your neighbors.

Zechariah 8:16

Set the oppressed free, share your food with the hungry, bring the poor into your house and clothe them. Then shall your light break forth like the morning.

Isaiah 58:6-8

Let justice well up as waters and righteousness as a mighty stream.

Amos 5:24

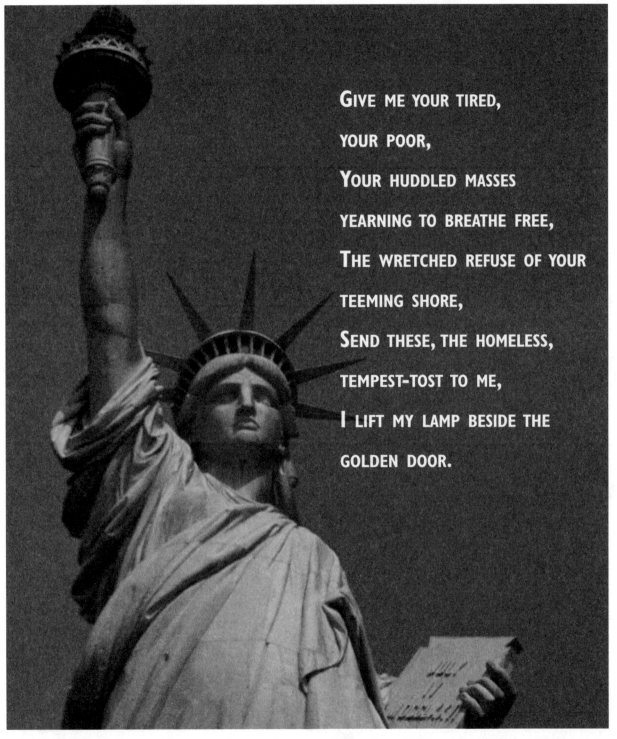

GIVE ME YOUR TIRED,

YOUR POOR,

YOUR HUDDLED MASSES

YEARNING TO BREATHE FREE,

THE WRETCHED REFUSE OF YOUR

TEEMING SHORE,

SEND THESE, THE HOMELESS,

TEMPEST-TOST TO ME,

I LIFT MY LAMP BESIDE THE

GOLDEN DOOR.

At the base of the Statue of Liberty is a poem written by Emma Lazarus. Her poem describes how the statue stands ready to welcome the poor and homeless who come to the shores of the United States. Read the quotations on the opposite page again. How might the teachings of the prophets have influenced this Jewish poet?

Can you write a poem based on the teachings of Zechariah, Jeremiah, or Malachi?

Isaiah's Dream

A verse from the Book of Isaiah is inscribed on a monument across the street from the United Nations building in New York City. It says:

And they shall beat their swords into ploughshares,
and their spears into pruning hooks;
Nation shall not lift up sword against nation,
neither shall they learn war anymore.

What Jewish value does this biblical verse teach?

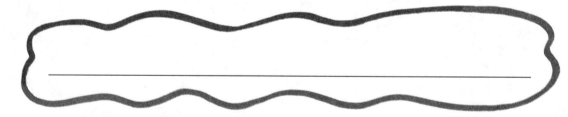

_____

Why do you think the members of the U.N. chose this quotation from *Nevi'im*?

_____

Turning Guns into Guitars

A modern Israeli poet, Yehudah Amichai, added his own ideas to Isaiah's dream. He wrote:

Don't stop after beating the swords into ploughshares, don't stop!
Go on beating and make musical instruments out of them.

What do you think is the best way to make sure we don't use weapons of war? Describe what the world would be like if your ideas came true.

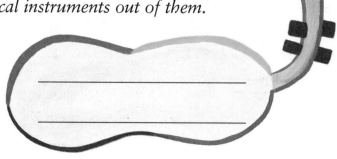

_____

_____

The Cup of Elijah

At the Passover *seder* a cup of wine is filled for Elijah the Prophet. Our tradition teaches that Elijah will announce the coming of the Messiah—the time when there will be peace, justice, and kindness throughout the world.

Some families fill the Cup of Elijah by adding wine from the cup of each person sitting at the table. They do this to show that the time of the Messiah will come only when everyone contributes to making the world a better place.

Fill Elijah's cup by writing your answers to these questions on the lines in the cup:

What two contributions do you plan to make now?
What two contributions would you like to make when you become an adult?

Be prepared to discuss why you think your contributions can improve the world.

Making the World A Better Place

Contributions to Make Now

1. _____

2. _____

Contributions to Make when I'm Older

1. _____

2. _____

47

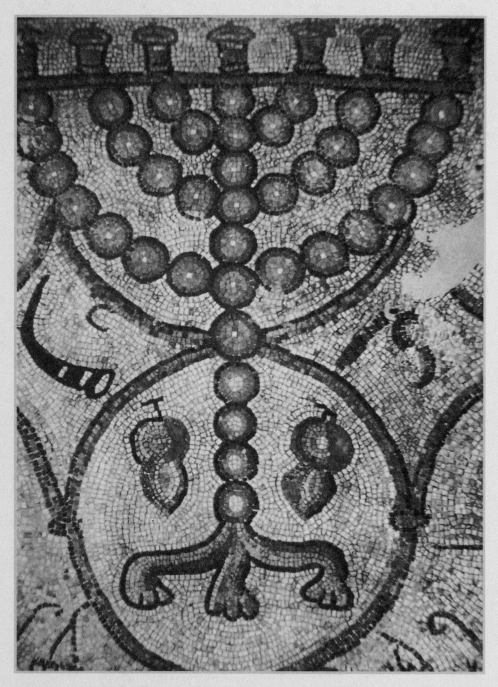

Mosaic art is made of small pieces of colored stone or glass. Joined together they form a picture. Imagine a mosaic picture of the world, complete and perfect. In it, God's creatures live in peace and harmony. The lamb lies next to the lion, and the beasts of the field, the birds of the sky, and the creatures that crawl on the ground roam in safety. There are no weapons of war, the deserts bloom with wildflowers, and all nations share the harvest of the fields.

What do you think the mosaic is made of? What could fill the world with justice and peace? God's *mitzvot* are the pieces of the mosaic, and it was our ancestors who first described the picture of holiness by teaching the *mitzvot*.

5

The Wisdom of God's Sages

Suppose you were told to mail a letter but you didn't know how to address the envelope or how much postage to put on. Could you do what you had been asked to do, or would you need some help?

In order to live as a holy nation, we need to know how to fulfill mitzvot. *For example, the Torah instructs us to celebrate the holiday of Sukkot by "living in booths for seven days." But how do we know how to build a sukkah? What materials to use? How high to build the walls and how to cover the roof?*

GOD'S FINEST STUDENTS

According to Jewish tradition, it was when our people received the Torah at Mount Sinai that we first dreamed of a world that was filled with justice and peace. The Bible explains that God later sent the prophets to teach us how to make our dream come true by living as a holy nation. The prophets taught us to love mercy and justice, to celebrate Shabbat and the holidays, and to understand the goodness of God's ways.

But we needed help in understanding exactly what to do—how to show mercy, pursue justice, celebrate holy days, and honor God. That help was given to us by the sages.

The rabbis of ancient times were God's finest students, sages such as Hillel and Shammai, and Rabbis Akiba, Meir, and Tarfon. They were dedicated to studying Torah and explaining its lessons to the Jewish people.

THE ANCIENT RABBIS

The Hebrew word *rabbi* comes from the word *rav*, meaning "teacher" or "master." It was first used after the days of the Holy Temple as a title of respect for the sages who explained God's laws so all Jews could understand and observe them.

The ancient rabbis did work similar to that of other people in their time. For example, Rabbi Akiba herded sheep and Rabbi Jonathan made shoes.

But when their workday was over, the sages came together to study God's laws and learn how the *mitzvot* can guide our behavior—how we should raise children, run businesses, build communities, and celebrate holy days.

At first, the rabbis passed their wisdom on by word of mouth, and that is why their teachings are sometimes called the Oral Law. But to make sure their wisdom was not lost, it was recorded by their students in a collection called the Talmud.

The Talmud contains Jewish law, or *halachah*. It records the discussions and opinions of the rabbis, and tells stories that explain how we can help complete God's world by living as an *am kadosh*, a holy people.

The sages were wise and pious, but they didn't always agree with one another. For example, Hillel and Shammai disagreed about how the Ḥanukkah *menorah* should be lit.

Shammai said that eight lights should be kindled on the first night and then one less on each of the following nights. Hillel said that on the first night one candle should be lit and additional candles lit on each night of the holiday.

Do we light the *menorah* according to Shammai's rule or Hillel's?

The rabbis teach us important truths and
provide a model of holiness we can follow.

It's a Mitzvah!

The great sage Hillel was once teaching a class when a young man wandered into the room.

"Each time you perform a *mitzvah*, you honor God," Hillel explained to his students. "With what *mitzvot* can you honor God today?"

"Visiting the sick, *bikkur ḥolim*," said one student.

"Praying with the community," called out a second.

"Reciting *Ha-Motzi* before eating," chimed in a third.

Hillel praised his students for their learning, then ended the lesson. As Hillel left the room, the stranger asked, "Where are you going?"

"To perform a *mitzvah* in the bathhouse," Hillel answered.

"What *mitzvah* could possibly be fulfilled there?" cried the young man in surprise.

"Bathing, of course," said Hillel.

"I don't understand," said the young man. "*Mitzvot* honor God. How does taking a bath honor God?"

"It's very simple," Hillel began. "Have you seen the statues of the king and queen in the city?" The young man nodded and Hillel continued. "Did you ever notice how well kept and clean they are, and wonder why they're treated so well?"

"Those statues are made in the image of royalty," the young man answered. "It would be disrespectful not to keep them clean."

"Of course," said Hillel. "And people are made in the image of even greater royalty. We are created in God's image—*b'tzelem Elohim.* Therefore, by keeping our bodies clean, we show respect for God. And that is why it is a *mitzvah* to take a bath!"

Why do you think we show respect for God when we provide homeless people with food and shelter? How do the healthful foods we eat and blessings we recite turn mealtime into holy time?

THE LESSONS OF THE RABBIS

The rabbis explained how workers should be treated with fairness and how, in turn, the workers must do the best job they can. For example, the rabbis said people must not be forced to work long hours. But they also ruled, "A person may not work in his own fields at night and in someone else's during the day, for if he does, his ability to serve his employer will be weakened."

The rabbis provide rules to help us build a *sukkah*. The walls may be made of any material, as long as they are strong enough to withstand the wind. The roof cannot be higher than 20 feet, and its covering must be thick enough so that the shade in the *sukkah* is greater than the sunlight. But we must be able to see the stars through the roof's branches at night.

The Fourth Commandment declares: "Observe Shabbat and keep it holy." The Bible says that for six days we shall work, but the seventh day shall be a day of rest. The rabbis help us understand the difference between "work" and "rest." For example, they explained that buying, selling, and writing are forms of work. They also explained that we add to the holiness of Shabbat by lighting candles, reciting *Kiddush*, and enjoying special meals.

Emergencies that require us to work can happen on Shabbat. Fires break out. People get hurt or sick and need help. The rabbis understood this and explained that a commandment can be broken to save a human life. Saving a life is called *pikuaḥ nefesh*, and it is permitted on Shabbat even if it requires us to violate a Shabbat law.

USING MODERN TECHNOLOGY TO FULFILL *MITZVOT*

We live in a world that is very different from our ancestors' world. "How," you ask, "can their teachings help us today?"

Yes, it's true that we live in a world of computers and jumbo jets. A world in which information can be sent from one continent to the next with a fax, or through the beam of a satellite. But like the generations before us, by studying the Bible and Talmud we can learn to use the talents and tools of our generation to fulfill *mitzvot*.

By learning the lessons of the sages and wise members of our generation, we can live as a holy people and do our part to make real our dream of a more just and peaceful world.

How can a cassette recorder or computer be used to observe the *mitzvah* of visiting the sick, *bikkur holim*? What household tools can be used to perform the *mitzvah* of honoring parents? A dishwasher? A vacuum cleaner? Or an old-fashioned broom?

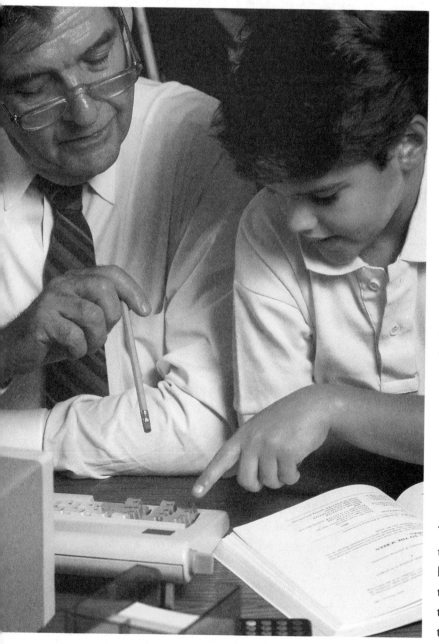

There was no electronic communication in the days of the sages—they lived almost 2,000 years ago. But had there been computers then, how might the rabbis have taught us to use them to perform *mitzvot*?

HEBREW LESSON

Talmud Torah

תַּלְמוּד תּוֹרָה

The Study of Holy Texts

When we study holy texts, such as the Torah, Prophets, and Talmud, it is as if we are talking with God and our sages. And through these conversations, we learn how Jewish law can guide our lives and help us live as an *am kadosh*.

A modern rabbi, Louis Finkelstein, said: "When I pray, I talk to God. When I study, God talks to me." How can studying our holy texts help you hear God's "voice"?

How can a TV be used to inform people of the need for volunteers to help victims of a hurricane? How can a radio be used to encourage people to give *tzedakah* to help families made homeless by a fire? How can a fax machine be used to provide help? What *mitzvot* can be performed with the help of a car? A truck? An airplane? Your two legs?

THE PURPOSE OF JEWISH LAW

The purpose of Jewish law is to improve the world. Therefore, Judaism often requires more of us than do the laws of our government.

For example, almost every country has laws that tell people not to hurt animals or steal. But Jewish law requires us to care for God's creations and to help those in need. Therefore, the rabbis explain, we are not only forbidden to hurt animals, we are also commanded to feed them before we eat. Not only are we forbidden to steal, we are also commanded to give *tzedakah* generously to the needy.

The purpose of most countries' laws is to create order in the land. The purpose of Jewish law is to help us live as an *am kadosh*, a holy people who work to improve the world.

When you follow Jewish law, you are being more than a good citizen. You are living as a partner with God. Each time you fulfill a *mitzvah*, you honor our Covenant and share in God's holiness by helping to create the mosaic picture our ancestors began long ago.

You Be the Judge

What is right or wrong according to Jewish law? You be the judge. Mark ✓ next to the behaviors you think follow Jewish law and X next to those you think break Jewish law. Be prepared to explain your decisions.

___ *Laughing at a classmate who makes a mistake*

___ *Forgiving a family member who teased you*

___ *Helping an older person carry a package*

___ *Reciting* Ha-Motzi *before you eat*

___ *Refusing to do an errand for a parent*

___ *Giving your bus seat to a person who has an injury*

___ *Attending a* seder *on Passover*

___ *Helping a friend study for a test*

___ *Pushing ahead of others on a movie line*

___ *Telephoning a classmate who is ill*

The Most Important Lesson

When asked to explain the Torah in one sentence, the sage Hillel responded, "Do not do to others what is hateful to you." A hundred years later, Rabbi Akiba taught that one of the most important lessons of the Torah is "to love your neighbor as yourself."

What is the most important Torah lesson you have learned so far in this book? Write it in one sentence on the banner below.

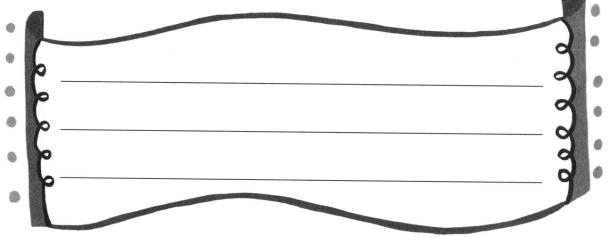

Mitzvah *Mosaic*

Many blessings, *brachot*, thank God for making us holy with *mitzvot*. For example, when we light candles on Shabbat and holidays we praise God for giving us the *mitzvah* of lighting candles. Words of thanks for God's commandments are also part of the *brachot* we recite before putting on a *tallit*, studying Torah, and affixing a *mezuzah*.

Why do you think our tradition teaches us to be grateful for the *mitzvot*?

The mosaic pieces below contain eight of God's commandments. Two pieces of the mosaic are empty. Write an additional *mitzvah* on each one.

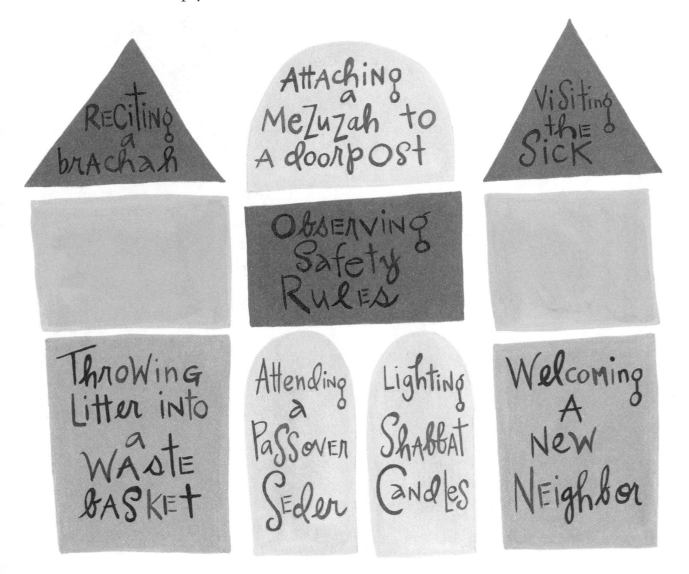

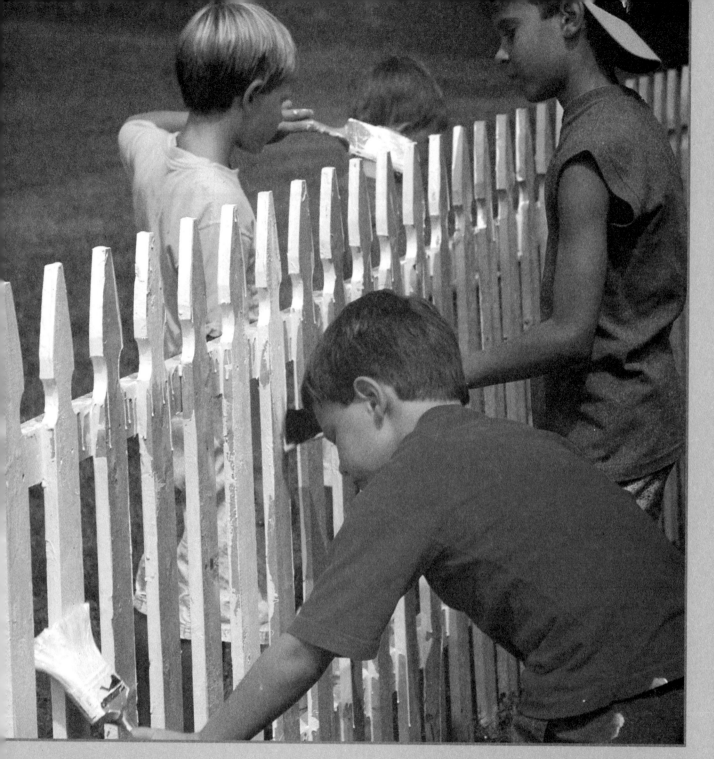

Eric's mother asked him to paint the picket fence around their house. He thought it would be boring, hard work. But when his younger brother and his friends Adam and Jonathan decided to help, the job became easier and fun. Have you ever faced a task that would have been difficult to complete by yourself? Working together, we can achieve what would be impossible for any one of us to do alone.

6

Joining God's Community

A hospital is a very busy place. Doctors and nurses help mothers give birth and care for people who are ill. There are pharmacists who supply medicine, people who cook, others who clean, volunteers who visit and entertain patients, and many other people who use their time, energy, and skills to help patients become healthy and strong. Do you think one person could do all the work? Why or why not?

THE GOAL OF THE JEWISH COMMUNITY

A group of people who live, work, study, pray, or play together is often called a community. Most people belong to several communities. For example, people may live with one group—their families—and study with another—their classmates.

Communities have goals. The goal of the Jewish community is to honor our partnership with God by living as an *am kadosh*, bringing more justice, mercy, and *shalom* to the world. This is a tradition passed down from God to Moses, from Moses to the prophets, from the prophets to the sages, and through the sages to us. We try to do our part, for no one person and no one generation can do it alone.

To succeed, we come together to study our holy texts, pray, celebrate, and offer help and comfort to those in need.

The members of this softball team and the other teams, coaches, and umpires in the league form a sports community. The goal of this team is to win the county championship this year. Can you describe two communities you belong to? What are the goals of those communities? How do you help them succeed in reaching their goals?

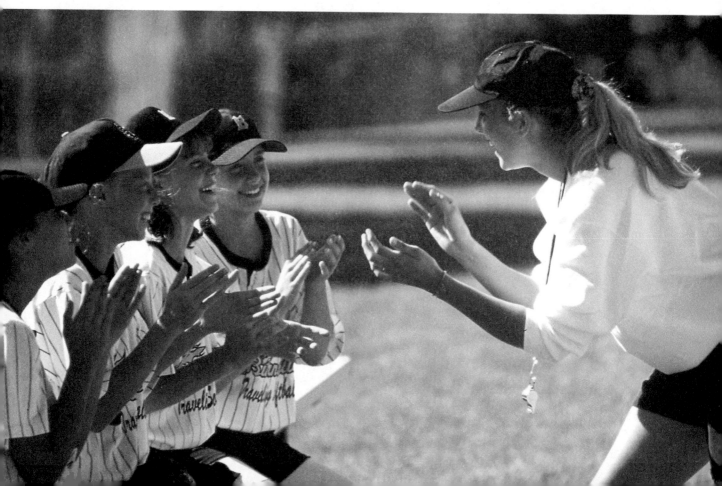

WE STUDY TORAH AS A COMMUNITY

Our sages taught that we all stood at Mount Sinai, that every Jewish soul that ever was and will be was present to hear God's voice and accept its share in the Covenant. When we study Torah together—rabbis, teachers, students, and families, in synagogues, schools, and homes—it is as if we are helping each other remember what we heard.

When we study together, we can contribute our ideas to the community and learn from the wisdom of others. We have the opportunity to share our love of God and Torah, and to be enriched by the love others have. What have you learned that you would like to teach others?

How can you and your classmates work together as a Jewish community to bring more holiness into your school and synagogue? Can you participate in Shabbat services? Make the building more attractive by painting a wall mural? What else can you do?

WE PRAY AS A COMMUNITY

Praying with our community reminds us that we are not alone—we are part of a much larger "family." Many Jewish prayers are intended to be said only when we pray in a *minyan*, a Jewish community made up of at least ten people who have reached the age of *bat* or *bar mitzvah*.

The sages believed that if we always prayed *by* ourselves, we might only pray *for* ourselves. They taught us to pray for what will add strength and holiness to the community, and to work in partnership with God and each other to make our prayers come true.

Certain prayers can be said only when we pray in a minyan. Two such prayers are *Kaddish* and *Kedushah*. Their names come from the Hebrew word *kadosh*, meaning "holy." When we recite these prayers, we are reminded of the importance of coming together as a community to live as a holy people—an am *kadosh*.

Working together isn't always easy, but without cooperation the Jewish people could never reach its goals.

The Human Ladder

Long ago, there was an island that floated in the middle of the sea. Once it had been a glorious place, surrounded by clear blue water and shady palm trees with plump, sweet dates. But since a terrible disease had come, the island was filled with despair.

One day, a magical bird perched atop the tallest tree. The islanders gathered in amazement as the bird spoke. "To end your suffering, one of you has only to touch the tip of my tail," it explained.

"I can do it!" young Esther Futterman called to the crowd. "But I need your help. Please stand on each other's shoulders and make a ladder for me to climb."

"Let me be the first rung in the ladder," said Lev the logger.

Climbing on his shoulders, Lev's wife Sarah cried out, "Who is ready to follow me?"

In a flash, Sonya the milkmaid stepped up, followed by her sisters Leah and Miriam. They were quickly joined by their friends David the doctor, Tuvia the tailor, and Berel the butcher.

Berel's six daughters—Bluma, Bina, Bella, Bayla, Batya, and Bracha—scrambled up after their father.

And last but not least, the entire Futterman family (there were eight Futtermans in all) made their way up the ladder, standing on one another's shoulders until Esther could almost reach the bird.

"If someone stands on tiptoes, I can touch the tail," she said softly.

"What?" bellowed Lev. "You want me to dance like a ballerina on my toes?"

"We've done what we can. How can you ask for more!" wailed Sonya and her sisters.

Before long, Berel and his six daughters were arguing among themselves, and the Futterman children were pinching and poking each other's toes.

The ladder began to twist and turn, swaying left then right.

"Enough already!" shouted Lev. "I no longer want to be part of this." And as he stepped away, everyone came tumbling down and the precious bird soared far beyond their reach.

If you could have spoken to the people in the story, what might you have said to help them work together? How would you have explained the importance of learning to discuss problems and differences of opinion rather than walking away in anger and frustration?

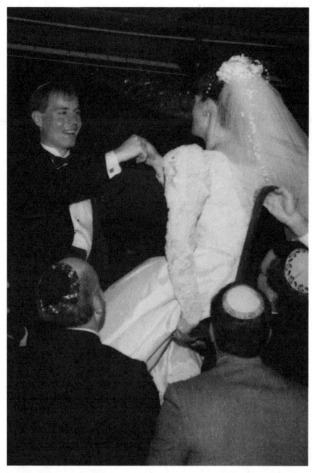

WE CELEBRATE AND OFFER COMFORT AS A COMMUNITY

Jewish tradition is filled with *mitzvot* of celebration—Shabbat, holidays, and joyous events, such as baby namings and confirmations. At these times, we come together to share our joy and to give thanks to God for the goodness in our lives.

In times of difficulty and sorrow, our community also comes together. We reach out to help others by fulfilling *mitzvot*. Through *tzedakah* projects we bring hot meals to elderly people, we visit the sick, work in soup kitchens to feed the poor, and comfort people whose loved ones have died. Through these holy acts, we remind each other of God's presence in the world.

Why do you think God commanded us to celebrate together, as well as to work together?

HEBREW LESSON

Klal Yisrael

כְּלַל יִשְׂרָאֵל

The Entire Jewish People

Klal Yisrael includes every single Jew without exception—every Jew in your family and neighborhood, every Jew in the country and the entire world. We are one people.

As *klal Yisrael*, we are taught to celebrate our many shared traditions, to be respectful of our differences, and to work together as partners with God.

THE JEWISH COMMUNITY IS ONE

The Jewish community stretches from one end of time to the other, from ancient days to the centuries ahead. By studying our holy texts and observing the *mitzvot*, you are connected to the Jewish community of our ancestors. And by passing our tradition on to the next generation, you remain connected to the Jewish community until the end of time.

The Jewish community circles the entire globe—from Shanghai to Tel Aviv, to London, Miami, and Toronto. Like you, Jews all over the world are part of the Covenant. Every Friday night, you can join all the Jews you will *ever* meet and all the Jews you will *never* meet by fulfilling the *mitzvot* of lighting candles and reciting *Kiddush* to welcome Shabbat. If you could visit any Jewish community in the world, you would find people studying the same Torah, praying to God in Hebrew, and facing Jerusalem as they recite the *Amidah*, just as you do.

Our tradition says that there are 600,000 letters in the Torah and there were 600,000 Israelites who stood at Sinai. From this we learn that just as each letter is required to complete the Torah, so each member of *klal Yisrael* is necessary to the community and has an important role in fulfilling our Covenant with God.

Building a Synagogue Community

Synagogues are more than the concrete, stone, or bricks from which they are built. They are holy places where our community gathers.

From the list below, select what you think goes into building a synagogue. Write one choice in each of the building blocks in the synagogue on the opposite page. Write three additional actions on the remaining blocks.

WHAT GOES INTO BUILDING A SYNAGOGUE?

- PRAYING TOGETHER
- DISCUSSING TORAH
- JUDGING OTHERS
- WORKING FOR *SHALOM*
- GOSSIPING
- WORKING TO STRENGTHEN ISRAEL
- WELCOMING STRANGERS

- CONTRIBUTING *TZEDAKAH*
- BEING UNFRIENDLY
- TREATING EVERYONE WITH RESPECT
- CELEBRATING SHABBAT AND HOLIDAYS
- COMFORTING ONE ANOTHER IN TIMES OF SADNESS

Write a message on the billboard below to welcome all Jews, *klal Yisrael*, to your synagogue.

_____

_____

_____

_____

PART TWO

Honoring Our Covenant with God

If I am not for myself, who will be for me? And if I am only for myself, what am I? And if not now, when?

Avot 1:14

The artist chooses paints from a pallet and with a brush applies color to the canvas to create a work of art. God's world is like an artist's pallet from which you can choose the colors of your life. The choices you make are your "brushstrokes." What *mitzvot* can you perform to make your life into a beautiful painting?

God Gives Us Free Will

God created great rivers and oceans whose waters flow across the earth, as well as insects, plants, and animals of every sort. But of the hundreds of thousands of God's creations, only human beings were given the ability to choose. Only human beings were given the gift of free will.

Our tradition teaches that because we have free will, we can choose how to live our lives. We can decide to make either good or bad choices. We can decide to share in God's holiness by observing the mitzvot, or to ignore the mitzvot and our Covenant with God.

Fire can bring warmth and light. It can heat nourishing food, warm shivering bodies, and brighten darkened rooms. But it also can destroy. If a flame touches the edge of a curtain or the dry leaves on the forest floor, it can spread and destroy everything in its path.

People can be like fire. We can be a source of goodness and warmth, or of destruction and hurt. But, unlike fire, people can make choices. What choices can you make to be a source of goodness and warmth?

"Why does God allow us to make such choices?" you may ask.

A very good question! People were given free will because without it we would be nothing more than slaves or puppets blindly following God's commands. If we couldn't choose to *ignore* the *mitzvot*, we also couldn't choose to *observe* them.

Just as a piece of cloth can be used to make either a *tallit* or a thief's mask, so our lives can be used for either holy or evil purposes. Sometimes the choice is not easy to make.

Jewish tradition teaches that there is no secret or trick to making good choices.

A Matter of Choice

Once, there was a boy named Simon who loved to play tricks on his older sister, Lucy. He would hide her homework, put salt in her cereal, and leave out the name of her caller when he wrote telephone messages.

On his way home from school one afternoon, Simon noticed a sparrow nesting in a nearby bush. He quickly grabbed the bird and walked up to his sister Lucy, who was standing near their house.

Holding the tiny bird behind his back, Simon said, "Lucy, I have a sparrow in my hands. Tell me, is it dead or alive?"

Now Lucy suspected that Simon wanted to trick her. Therefore, she reasoned, the bird must be alive. For if it were dead, and she said so, there was nothing Simon could do to prove her wrong.

But if the bird were alive and she said so, Simon might crush it just to prove her wrong.

Lucy wanted Simon to spare the bird's life and she also wanted to teach him an important lesson. So when Simon said, "Give me your answer. Is the bird dead or alive?" Lucy replied, "I do not know, for the answer is in your hands."

Our tradition teaches us to choose life by following God's ways. If you could speak to Simon, what would you say to help him make that choice?

It's not always easy to make good choices—particularly when we must choose between two important activities. For example, do we go to baseball practice or prepare for a piano lesson? If we plan ahead, is it possible to do both?

What difficult choices have you had to make? What helps you make good choices?

You Can Count on Mitzvot

It's human for our feelings to change. Sometimes we feel cheerful and, at other times, upset or sad. Because feelings change, we can't always rely on them to help us make good choices. But we can always count on the commandments.

Tzedakah is the *mitzvah* to give to those in need, even when we feel stingy. *Achilat matzah* is the *mitzvah* to eat *matzah* on Passover, even when we feel like eating bread. And *gemilut ḥassadim* is the *mitzvah* to act with kindness, even when we feel nasty.

Think about it. Have you ever been tempted to play a mean trick on someone, peek at a classmate's test paper, or take something that wasn't yours? Did you think about how unkind or dishonest it would be but still feel like doing it?

COMMUNITY HELPS US MAKE GOOD CHOICES

Our tradition teaches that by studying, working, praying, and celebrating with the Jewish community, we can help each other make good choices. When we study Torah together, we remind each other to honor the Covenant by observing *mitzvot*. When we work together on *bikkur ḥolim* and *tzedakah* projects, such as visiting sick people in hospitals and bringing food and clothes to the poor, we support each other in the good choices we make and we share the joy of following God's ways. And when we pray and celebrate together, we are reminded that our good choices help us complete the world by living as an *am kadosh*.

THE CHOICES YOU MAKE ARE IMPORTANT

Our sages taught that our lives are like books in which we record what we want remembered about us. This means we are the "authors" of our own lives.

Every day we fill another page with the choices we've made, the stories of our lives. They can be wonderful stories of hard work and celebration, love and kindness, honesty and fairness. And like the beauty of a Shabbat flame, our stories can add light to the world.

Your Book of Life

Each time you make a choice about how to treat yourself and others, your decision leads to another story in your Book of Life. What are some of your stories? What good choices have you made even when doing so has been difficult? For example, were you able to tell the truth even when it was tempting to lie, or take the time to help others even when it was easier to ignore them? How and what have you learned from your mistakes?

What story would you like to add to your Book of Life in the future? What choices will you have to make so that story can come true? Write them in the book below.

It's All in the Balance

The sages teach us the importance of creating balance in our lives through the performance of *mitzvot*. To keep the scales in balance, on the left side list four *mitzvot* you can perform to add happiness and health to your own life. On the right side of the scale list four *mitzvot* you can perform to add goodness and joy to the rest of Creation.

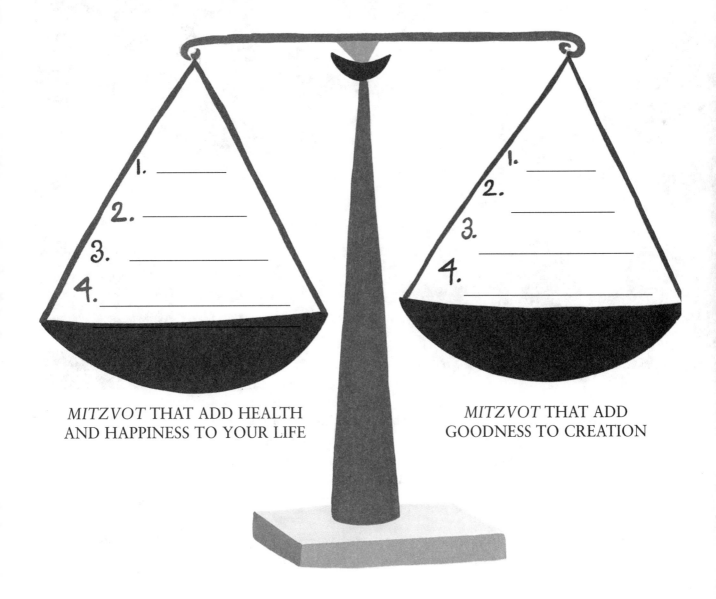

MITZVOT THAT ADD HEALTH
AND HAPPINESS TO YOUR LIFE

MITZVOT THAT ADD
GOODNESS TO CREATION

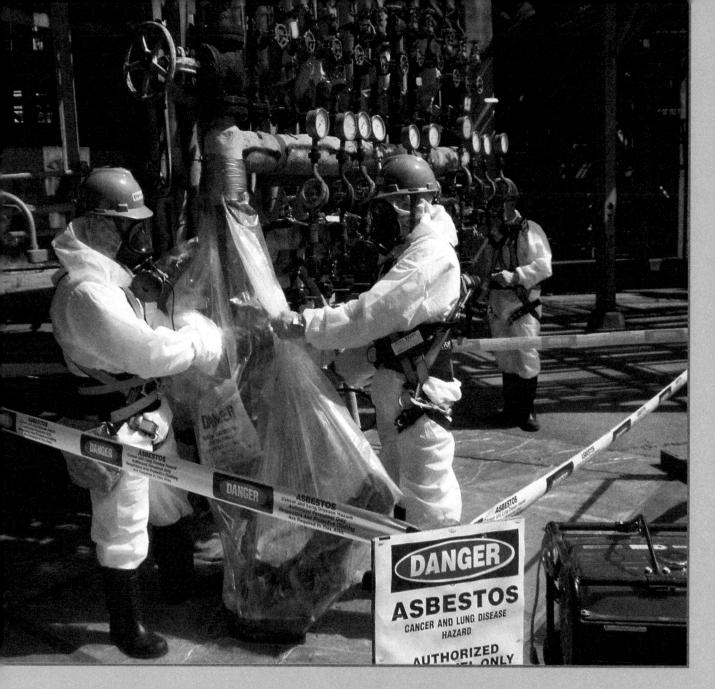

Asbestos is a mineral that is strong and flexible. It doesn't burn, or easily conduct heat or electricity. The ancient Egyptians used it for making cloth and in modern times it has been used in thousands of manufactured products, such as floor and ceiling tiles, cement, and fireproof clothing.

Until recently, no one knew that when asbestos is inhaled, it can cause lung disease and cancer. Laws were passed to control its continued use and the long, dangerous, and costly process of asbestos removal began.

Do you think we are required to repair damage we have caused even when—in the beginning—we didn't know that our actions would bring harm? Why or why not?

Repairing God's World

Do you know the blessing that is recited over bread, Ha-Motzi? We say: Blessed are You, Adonai our God, Ruler of the universe, who brings forth bread from the earth.

What does the blessing mean? Do loaves of ḥallah grow in the ground? Does God plant corn muffins and frankfurter rolls? Does God "bring forth bread" without our help? Could we do it by ourselves?

Let's think about it. After all, we are partners with God. How does the partnership work?

Like the boy in this photograph, many children don't have shoes to protect their feet from the hard rocky ground, beds to sleep in at night, or enough food to eat. Parents try to give their children what they need, but they don't always succeed. Sometimes wars separate families, and sometimes droughts or other natural disasters make it impossible to grow crops or raise cattle.

Why do you think our tradition teaches that it is our responsibility to help such people?

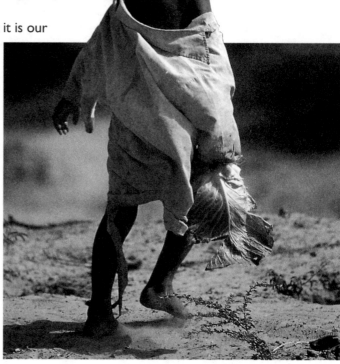

God doesn't create loaves of bread. God provides resources such as seeds, soil, air, sunshine, and rain, from which wheat can grow. People do their part by planting the seeds, harvesting the wheat, grinding it into flour, and preparing and baking the dough. In addition, Judaism teaches that it is our responsibility to make sure God's resources are used to benefit everyone.

Not only are we required to share a portion of our food with those who are hungry, it is also our duty to help them grow their own. That is why it is a *mitzvah* to work with others to irrigate land in countries suffering from drought, and to teach developing nations how to renew soil and protect crops from insects and disease.

Without the Bible and Talmud there would be no instructions for *tikkun olam*. Without community we would have no one to work with to make our dream of a better world come true.

REPAIRING AND IMPROVING THE WORLD

Our sages taught that people were created to enjoy and care for the world. We study the wisdom of the Torah, Prophets, and Talmud to learn how to repair damage when it occurs. By doing our share, we participate in a very important part of Jewish life called *tikkun olam*—repairing the world.

FINDING OPPORTUNITIES FOR *TIKKUN OLAM*

On any day of the week, you will hear or see many signals for *tikkun olam*. Pay attention! If someone is teased in class or on the playground, don't join in. Offer a word of kindness. When you see someone carrying heavy packages, or someone stumble and fall, don't look the other way. Provide a helping hand. When you are finished eating, don't leave a mess. Clean up after yourself.

Our tradition teaches us to care for God's creations. To teach children this important lesson, our sages tell a story about the first person, Adam.

One day, as Adam tried to pick some cherries, the branch they hung from pulled itself high above his reach. The very same thing happened when he went to the plum, peach, and pear trees. Finally, Adam realized that people cannot take without giving. So he watered the trees and pruned their dead branches. The next time Adam reached for a ripe fruit, the branch lowered before him as if to shake his hand.

What opportunities do you have to give to God's other creations? In what ways do these creations give to you?

You don't have to wait until you're an adult to make a difference in the world. As a member of the Covenant, you too have the responsibility of *tikkun olam*.

Perhaps you can tutor a younger student like the girl in the picture, or run errands for a neighbor who is ill.

Talk about these and other opportunities with friends and teachers. Together, you can find ways to add goodness to the world.

There are times when the evil acts of others bring darkness to the world. What can we do to repair the damage they have caused?

Let There Be Light

The story is told of a rabbi whose students asked him how to rid the world of evil and injustice. "Tell us how to remove this darkness from the Earth," they begged.

"Let us seek the answer in the cellar," the rabbi said.

He handed every student a candle and led them down the wooden stairs. The students wondered why their teacher was taking them to such a dark and cold place.

Then the rabbi lit his own candle. It was still dark. But when he used that candle to light everyone else's, the basement became filled with light.

Then the rabbi explained, "Do not despair over evil and injustice. Instead, work together to remove it from God's world. Just as God brought light into the world through Creation, so we can bring light through our acts of *tikkun olam*."

How can the *mitzvah* of *tzedakah* add "light" to the world? The *mitzvah* of apologizing for hurtful acts? What other *mitzvot* can add light to God's world?

THE GOLDEN RULE

During synagogue services, we pray for the day when God's laws will be followed by all people, for the time when peace will fill the world. Through acts of *tikkun olam*, we become partners with God in making our prayers come true.

A man once challenged the great sage Hillel, who lived 2,000 years ago. He said, "If you can teach me the entire Torah while I stand on one foot, I'll convert to Judaism." Hillel answered, "Do not do to others what you do not want them to do to you. This is the entire Torah. The rest is commentary—an explanation of that rule. Now go and study Torah."

Hillel's answer is sometimes called the Golden Rule. Do you think the world would be a better place if more people observed the Golden Rule? Why or why not?

Are you surprised by Hillel's answer? Are you wondering why it takes so many years of study to become a *bar* or *bat mitzvah* if the entire Torah can be taught in one sentence?

Think about it. While Hillel was able to teach the Torah in one sentence, could someone learn the wisdom of Torah by *hearing* just one sentence? Why?

HEBREW LESSON

Tikkun Olam

תִּקּוּן עוֹלָם

The Repair of the World

The Hebrew word *tikkun* means "repair" and "strengthen." When we do the work of *tikkun olam*, we repair and strengthen our caring relationships with people and with the rest of God's Creation. Sometimes these relationships have been damaged by anger, selfishness, or disrespect. Sometimes they need to be strengthened because we've paid too little attention to them.

EVIL AND INJUSTICE IN GOD'S WORLD

People often blame God for allowing suffering in the world. But we are God's partners—what is *our* responsibility?

Suffering can be caused by acts of human evil. For example, war often brings the killing of innocent people as well as the bombing of homes and towns. We can work to prevent such cruelty because people have free will. We can choose to do what is good by working to end the evil acts of others.

▲▲▲▲▲▲▲▲▲▲▲▲▲▲▲▲▲▲▲▲▲▲▲▲▲

How can people put an end to the cruelty of war? The injustice of poverty? The evil of starvation?

In every generation, people have asked why God permits the pain caused by disease and natural disasters such as earthquakes and floods. No one, not even the greatest sage, has been able to answer such questions. The truth is, we simply don't know. But even if we never understand, we are not helpless. For instance, how could you and your classmates help victims of a flood? Could you raise money or run a clothing drive?

Some suffering is caused by illness, disease, or acts of nature. We can work to lessen such suffering. For example, with the help of modern science, we can warn people of a coming storm that may do damage or take lives. We can use medical skills to heal sickness and injuries and, when we see suffering, we can reach out and help through other acts of *tikkun olam*. Just like the prophet Isaiah who heard God's call, we can say, "Here I am! *Hineni!*" I am God's partner and I want to do my part to repair and complete the world.

WE ARE EACH ASKED TO DO OUR PART

In ancient times, Rabbi Tarfon taught, "It is not your responsibility to complete the task, but neither are you free from doing your part."

Jewish heroes are people who do their part to improve the world. They are members of our community—our rabbis, our teachers, our neighbors, and our friends. They are people just like you.

Our tradition teaches us to use our knowledge, skills, and money to help those who are ill, as well as to recite a prayer asking for God's help.

Why do you think both action and prayer are required? Why do we need both technology and a prayerbook to repair the world?

Modern Jewish Heroes

Each generation of our people has its heroes—righteous men and women who dedicate their lives to the creation of a better world through the *mitzvot*.

JONAS SALK (1914-1995)
Jonas Salk received the Presidential Citation and Congressional Medal for Distinguished Achievement for his many contributions to public health *(pikuaḥ nefesh)*. His discovery of the vaccine against polio saved thousands of children's lives.

ABRAHAM JOSHUA HESCHEL (1907-1972)
Fulfilling the *mitzvah* of study *(talmud Torah)* taught Rabbi Abraham Joshua Heschel how to make the world a better place for all people. He fought for the civil rights of African Americans and for the freedom of oppressed Jews in what was then called the Soviet Union.

LILLIAN WALD (1867-1940)
Lillian Wald pursued justice *(tzedek)* by relieving human suffering. She brought health care to the poor and fought for laws to protect the rights of children.

GOLDA MEIR (1898-1978)
Love of Israel *(ahavat Tziyon)* inspired Golda Meir to settle in *Eretz Yisrael*. There she worked to establish the Jewish state and became the fourth Prime Minister of Israel in 1969.

YITZHAK RABIN (1922-1995)

A military commander who became Prime Minister of Israel, Yitzhak Rabin heeded the words of Isaiah. He was a pursuer of peace *(rodef shalom)* by talking with his enemies so they might learn to live together.

HENRIETTA SZOLD (1860-1945)

Henrietta Szold was a schoolteacher who, through many acts of loving-kindness *(gemilut ḥassadim)*, helped save thousands of children from the cruelty of the Nazis in World War II. Working with others, she brought the children to *Eretz Yisrael* to rebuild their lives and the Land.

HANNAH SENESH (1921-1944)

A poet and paratrooper, Hannah Senesh lived a life of creativity and courage *(ometz lev)*. In 1944, while on a mission to save Jews from the Holocaust, Hannah was arrested and executed by the Nazis.

Many Jewish heroes aren't famous, but *all* perform *mitzvot*. In the frame above, write a "portrait" of someone you know— a friend, teacher, or relative—who is a hero by describing the *mitzvot* the person fulfills.

Tikkun Olam *Alert!*

When we pay attention to the world around us, we notice not only signs of
God's presence, such as the beauty of nature and the kindness of people, but also
the opportunities to share in God's holiness by performing acts of *tikkun olam*.

List three signs that can alert you to the need for *tikkun olam*. For example,
someone who is having difficulty learning a sport or subject at school, someone
who needs help crossing a street, or a pet who is hungry. Explain how, through
your actions, you can say, "*Hineni*, I'm here to help!"

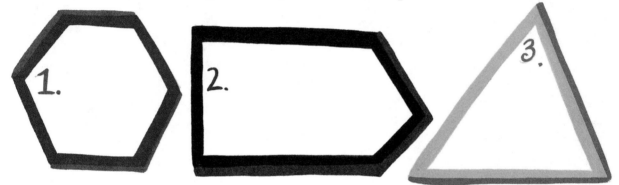

Add the Brightness of Your Light

As God brought light into the world
through Creation, you can add light
through acts of *tikkun olam*. Light
the candles by writing an act of
tikkun olam you can perform at
home, school, and synagogue.

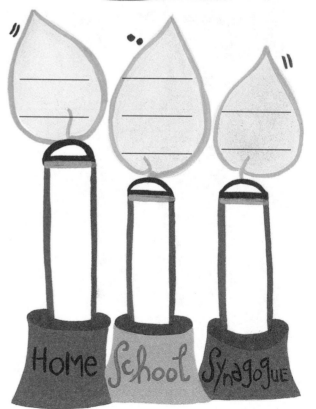

Caring Connections

Fill in *mitzvot* that create caring connections between people and help make the world complete.

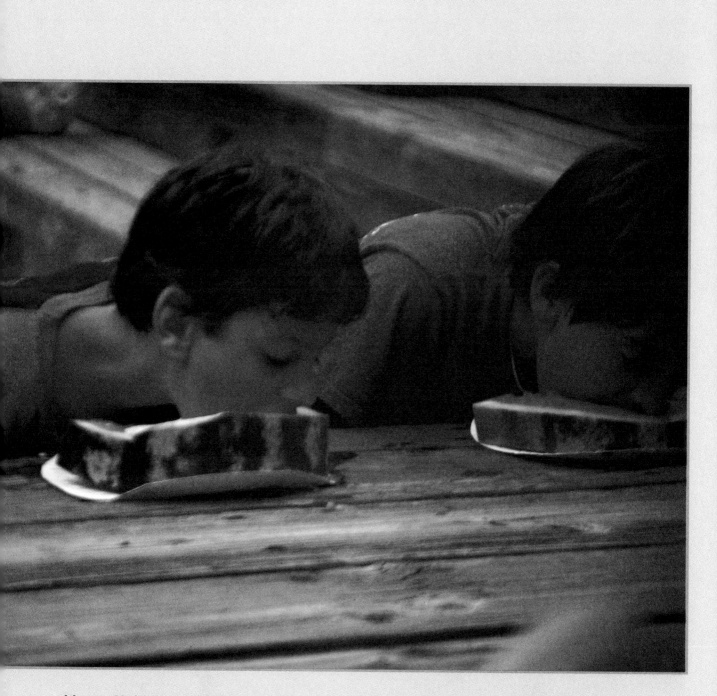

It's over 90 degrees and fruit never tasted as sweet and juicy as it does at this watermelon-eating contest! What fruits refresh you on a hot summer day? How do God's other creations help you enjoy a life of good health and fun? How about the warmth of the sun or a down jacket on a cold winter day?

Reciting *brachot* that thank God for the wonders of Creation reminds us to behave as responsible guests in God's world.

9

Caring for God's World

How would you feel if guests stayed at your house and, instead of showing appreciation for your hospitality, ruined everything in sight? Suppose they let food spoil by not putting it in the refrigerator, broke dishes and furniture, and spilled hot chocolate on the living room rug.

In what ways do people sometimes behave like rude guests in God's world? Do we have the duty to take care of what God created? What are our responsibilities as partners with God and members of the Covenant?

WE ARE THE CARETAKERS OF CREATION

Judaism teaches that all of nature belongs to God and that people were created to enjoy its goodness and to care for it. Many of the blessings we recite thank God for creating the wonders of nature. For example, we thank God for the food we eat when we recite *Ha-Motzi*, and for the fragrance of spices and the light of fire when we say *Havdalah* at the end of Shabbat. We can also praise God for rainbows and thunder in the *brachot* we recite.

Nature's wonders include insects and wildlife—spiders, bees, tigers, and whales. They also include natural resources, such as oceans, forests, and the air we breathe. All these creations make up our environment. As partners with God, we have the responsibility to show kindness to God's other creatures and to use Earth's natural resources wisely so future generations can enjoy the same gifts we do.

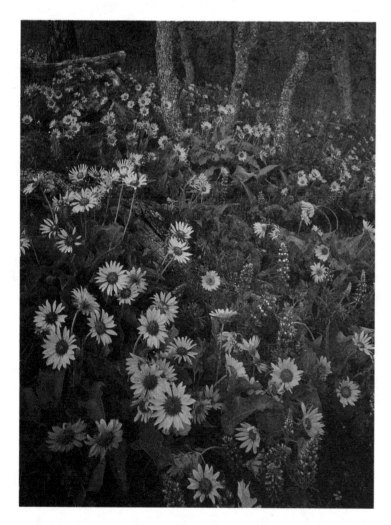

Have you ever been tempted to pick flowers you saw growing in a park or in the countryside? Have you thought, "No one will miss a few"? But if everyone picked just one flower, it wouldn't be long before there were none left to enjoy.

If you want a bouquet of flowers, you can buy them from someone who has raised flowers for the purpose of cutting and selling them, or you can plant your own. How can you use a camera or a paintbrush to bring flowers home from a park? How can you use pen and paper?

One way of making sure that future generations
enjoy the same wonders of nature we do is to limit
our use of these precious resources.

The Goat that Made the Stars Sing

Long ago the night sky was filled with beautiful music. This was due
to a most extraordinary goat.

This goat had horns so long that their tips brushed the sky and tickled
the heavens until the stars twinkled and sang songs of great delight.
Lulled to sleep by this beautiful music, even babies and fierce wolves
slept peacefully through the night.

One day as the goat was grazing in a field, a young man passed by.
"Hello, my friend," called out the goat. "What brings you here today?"

"I need a small box in which to place a ring for my beloved. Might I
snip off a small piece of your horn from which to make the box?"

"Of course, dear friend," said the goat.

And so the young man clipped a small piece of horn and carved a box from it. When he returned to his village, his friends insisted, "We want such boxes, too."

Only one friend held back. She warned, "If each of you takes a piece, the goat's horns will no longer reach the sky."

But the villagers thought only of their pleasure. They ran to the goat, and one by one, clipped a piece of horn.

When nightfall came, the villagers went to bed feeling quite pleased with themselves and their beautiful boxes. But their satisfaction quickly faded. For the only sounds they heard that night—and every night thereafter—were the fierce howls of wolves and the frightened wails of babies.

Do you think all the people in the story needed boxes? If they did, what could they have used instead of the goat's horn?

Have you or your classmates ever left a table in the school cafeteria looking like this? What might the people who left this mess have done to show concern for other people and for the environment?

DO NOT WASTE!

Jewish law commands us not to destroy, *bal tash'ḥit*! For example, we are forbidden to destroy the fruit trees of our enemies—even during a war—or to change a stream's course if doing so will cause plants or crops to die. Jewish law also forbids us to be wasteful of our possessions. When we waste food or carelessly destroy household goods, such as dishes and furniture, we are breaking the law of *bal tash'ḥit*.

Why do you think being wasteful is against God's law? How can you observe the *mitzvah* of *bal tash'ḥit* by taking better care of your clothing, books, and sports equipment?

Unfortunately, people are sometimes careless or greedy and do not always use natural resources responsibly. Then all God's creatures suffer the consequences. What happens to fish and birds when people spill oil or dump garbage in the ocean? To insects and animals when forests are destroyed by fires caused by careless campers?

We are guests in God's world and are responsible for its care.

▲◢▲◢▲◢▲◢▲◢▲◢▲◢▲◢▲◢▲◢▲◢▲◢

It's a privilege to borrow books from the library. We earn the privilege when we take care of what we borrow and return it undamaged so that others can enjoy it after us.

What can you do to take care of your library books? How can you take care of the environment so that future generations can enjoy the same resources you do?

The Torah teaches us that an animal should not be separated from its mother until it is at least seven days old. The Talmud goes on to explain that before buying an animal, we must buy food for it.

Why do you think our tradition teaches us to treat animals with kindness and concern?

SHOWING COMPASSION TO ANIMALS

Has a kitten ever jumped on your lap, eager to share affection? Or has a friendly dog brightened your day with a welcoming wag of its tail? What did you do when something like this happened?

Judaism teaches us to show our appreciation for all animals by observing the *mitzvah* of being concerned for *tza'ar ba'alei ḥayyim*, "the pain of all that lives." Our sages told a story, or *midrash*, to help us understand the importance of this *mitzvah*.

One day, while Moses was tending a flock of sheep, a baby lamb scampered away. Moses chased after it until he saw it stop at a stream. "I didn't know you ran away because you were thirsty, little one. You must also be tired now," said Moses. He waited patiently for the lamb to finish drinking and then picked it up and carried it back to the flock.

God was pleased and said to Moses, "Because you showed compassion to the lamb, you will tend My flock, the People of Israel."

What do you think the rabbis wanted to teach us? How can showing compassion to animals help you live as a partner with God?

The laws of many countries make it illegal to be cruel to animals, but they do not require people to show compassion by helping animals in need. Jewish law, or *halachah*, does require us to be compassionate. For example, we are required to provide a cold and hungry animal with shelter and food, and we must feed our pets before we feed ourselves. Do you think Jewish law permits us to hunt animals for sport? Why or why not?

USING OUR KNOWLEDGE FOR GOOD

Our knowledge of science can help us find new ways to observe the *mitzvot* of *bal tash'ḥit* and being concerned for *tza'ar ba'alei ḥayyim*. For example, we can recycle plastic, glass, and paper. Science can also show us how to renew soil that has lost water and minerals so that wheat and corn can grow once again. And scientific knowledge can help us make medicines that heal people and animals who are ill.

But our knowledge of science can also be used to damage God's world. We can use our knowledge to manufacture products that pollute the air and soil, create illness, and destroy life.

This is why our knowledge of science is not enough. We need to study the Bible and Talmud to learn *how* to use the knowledge we gain through science. For it is God's law, not science, that teaches us the difference between good and evil. It is God's law that teaches us to treat Creation in ways that are holy.

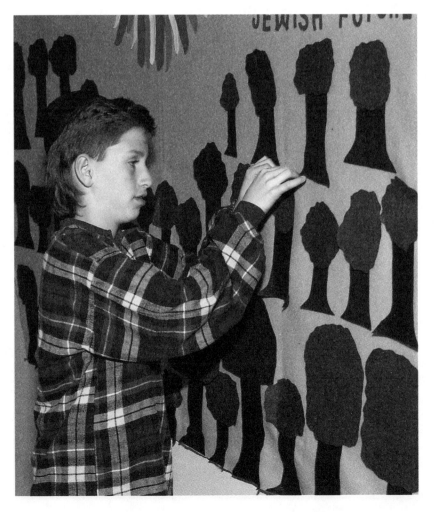

On Tu B'Shevat we celebrate the birthday of trees. One way to observe the holiday is to plant trees at home. Another is to donate money to the Jewish National Fund so that trees can be planted in Israel to restore the land and protect the natural resources for future generations. That's what this boy did. He is marking his gift by hanging a drawing of a tree on the school bulletin board.

Learning from Creation

The Book of Job teaches:

> *The beasts that walk on land will instruct you,*
> *The birds that fly above will tell you,*
> *And the earth and fish will speak to you*
> *Of the greatness of God's Creation.*

Draw a cartoon that shows an animal that walks on "all fours," or a bird or a fish. Inside the speech balloon, write what the creature tells us about the greatness of God's Creation. For example, a duck might tell us how its down provides us with warm coats and quilts, or a cow might tell us how its milk helps make our teeth and bones strong.

Trees Protect and Feed Us

Our sages taught that we must plant trees because they protect the Earth and all the creatures who live on it. Trees provide food, homes, and shade for many of God's creatures. They add oxygen to the air and are used in making medicines for people and animals.

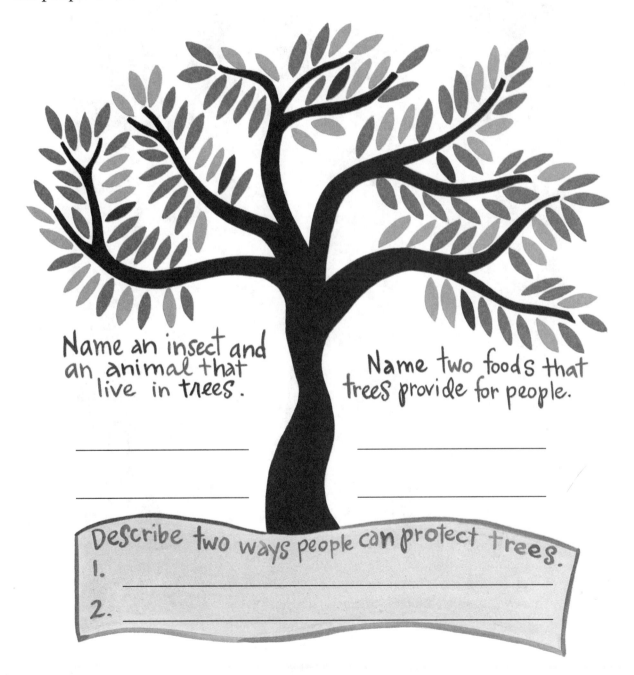

Name an insect and an animal that live in trees.

_____

_____

Name two foods that trees provide for people.

_____

_____

Describe two ways people can protect trees.

1. _____

2. _____

On Purim we read the *Megillah*. It tells how, long ago, the Jewish community in Persia was saved from destruction. Today we dress in costumes to help us remember Esther and Mordecai's courage and loyalty to God.

What other Jewish holidays celebrate important events in the history of our people? How do they teach us about what is holy?

10

God Makes Time Holy

Did you ever read a book or see a movie about people who traveled back in time or forward to the future? Perhaps they traveled to ancient cities and met with great kings and queens. Or maybe they traveled to the future to see how people will live in centuries to come.

Did you know that traveling through time is an important part of Jewish life? As Jews, we often travel back in time and forward to the future because such traveling helps us do our best to live as partners with God in the present.

We travel back in time at the Passover *seder*. We remember how God brought us out of slavery in Egypt and gave us the Torah so we could follow God's ways and become an *am kadosh*.

JEWISH TIME TRAVEL

On Passover we make a *seder* and read the *Haggadah*. In this way, we travel back in time through our people's memory of the Exodus and observe the commandment to consider ourselves as personally having been delivered from slavery by God.

On Shavuot we travel back to Mount Sinai and the giving of the Torah by reading the Ten Commandments. The words of Torah remind us that we stood together at Sinai when God and Moses spoke to us all.

On Ḥanukkah, when we light candles, we travel back to the days of the Holy Temple, the *Bet Ha-Mikdash*. We remember how God's presence gave the small band of Maccabees courage to defend Israel against a great army.

On these holidays and others, we travel back in time to remember how God's presence has been like an out-stretched arm guiding us through history. Passover reminds us that it was God who delivered our people from slavery. Shavuot reminds us that God gave each and every one of us the gift of Torah. And Ḥanukkah reminds us that God's holy presence is a source of courage and strength.

On Jewish holy days, our hearts and minds also travel to the future, to the time when our Covenant with God

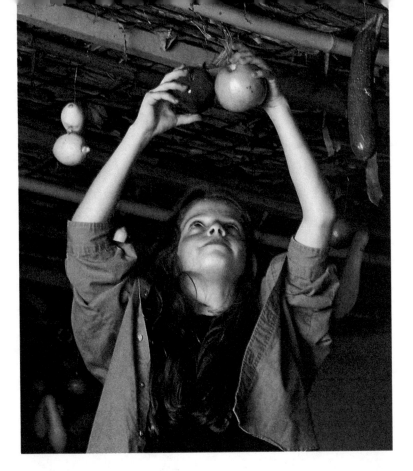

Building and decorating a *sukkah* reminds us of ancient days when our people built tiny huts to provide shelter in the wilderness. When we eat in the *sukkah*, we remember how God fed us with manna as we journeyed toward the Promised Land.

On the festival of Sukkot, how can remembering the mercy God showed us in the past remind you to do your part to feed and shelter those who need help today?

will be fulfilled and *shalom* will embrace the world.

Our vision, or dream, of the future reminds us that the prophets said our observance of holidays pleases God only if we also make an effort to become better people.

That is why on Passover we not only enjoy eating the *seder* meal and finding the *afikoman*, we also remember to work for the freedom of all people. That is why on Shavuot we not only read the Ten Commandments and decorate our homes and the synagogue with flowers, we also remember to observe the *mitzvot* of *tzedakah* and *sh'lom bayit*, family peace. And that is why on Ḥanukkah we not only light candles and eat crispy *latkes*, we also remember to fight for justice for our people and for others.

▲▲

Rosh Hashanah is also called Yom Ha-Zikaron, which means "The Day of Remembering." On the Jewish New Year we remember the choices we made in the past year and consider if we must make better ones in the future.

What does Rosh Hashanah teach us about the purpose of remembering? Do you think remembering can be a holy act? Why or why not?

Our Jewish Year at a Glance

These are some of the holidays we celebrate each year. Some are ancient holidays that we were commanded to celebrate from the days of the Bible. Some are modern holidays that we began to observe in the 20th century. Each has its own stories and traditions, but all have the same purpose—to remind us of what is important so we can honor our Covenant with God.

fall

Tishre 1
ROSH HASHANAH (רֹאשׁ הַשָּׁנָה)
The Jewish New Year

Tishre 10
YOM KIPPUR (יוֹם כִּפּוּר)
Day of Atonement

Tishre 15
SUKKOT (סֻכּוֹת)
Autumn Harvest Festival

Tishre 22/23
SIMḤAT TORAH (שִׂמְחַת תּוֹרָה)
Celebration of Completion of the Year's Torah Reading

Kislev 25
Ḥanukkah (חֲנֻכָּה)
The Festival of Lights Celebrating the Victory of the Maccabees

winter

Shevat 15
TU B'SHEVAT (ט"וּ בִּשְׁבָט)
The New Year of the Trees

Adar 14
PURIM (פּוּרִים)
Celebration of the Survival of Our People in Ancient Persia

spring

Nisan 15
PASSOVER (פֶּסַח)
Celebration of Our Deliverance from Slavery in Ancient Egypt

Nisan 27
YOM HASHOAH (יוֹם הַשׁוֹאָה)
Memorial to the Six Million Jews Killed in the Holocaust

Iyar 5
YOM HA'ATZMA'UT (יוֹם הָעַצְמָאוּת)
Israel Independence Day

Sivan 6
SHAVUOT (שָׁבוּעוֹת)
Spring Harvest Festival and Anniversary of the Giving of the Torah

summer

Av 9
TISHA B'AV (תִּשְׁעָה בְּאָב)
Day of Mourning for the Destruction of the First and Second Temples

105

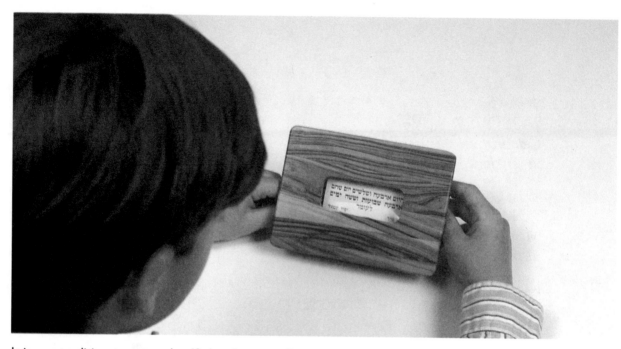

It is our tradition to count the 49 days between Passover and Shavuot, the holiday that celebrates the giving of the Torah. An *omer* calendar, like the one shown here, is often used to keep track of each day. Have you ever counted the days to a special event, such as your birthday or a family trip? How did you feel as the event drew closer? How do you think our ancestors felt as they stood at Mount Sinai?

THE ISLAND IN TIME

Can you think of a holiday that comes at the end of every week, all year long? That's right, it's Shabbat!

Some people think that because Shabbat comes so often, it is less important than other Jewish holidays. But the opposite is true. The Torah teaches that Shabbat is a sign of our Covenant with God, and our sages taught that observing Shabbat is equal to fulfilling all the other commandments. Why do you think that stopping our daily work and joining our community in prayer can remind us of our Covenant with God?

Our tradition teaches that Shabbat is like an *Island in Time*. What do you think this means? How can you celebrate Shabbat as a holy day—separate from and more wonderful than the other days of the week?

It's wonderful to be able to go to school and learn new things. But can you imagine what it would be like to be in school 7 days a week for 365 days a year! Then you would be a slave, just as our ancestors were slaves in ancient Egypt. This is one reason why Shabbat is such an important day.

HOLY TIME CONNECTS US TO GOD AND TO OTHER JEWS

Shabbat and the other holidays are also reminders that each of us is connected both to God and to other Jews, *klal Yisrael*.

If you could visit any Jewish community in the world, you would find people dancing with Torah scrolls on Simḥat Torah just as you do and welcoming Shabbat with the same words you recite. On Passover too they sit down to a *seder*, and on Purim they also dress up as Esther and Mordecai.

If you could take a time machine to another period—past or future—and visit a Jewish community there, those Jews would invite you to join them in observing the *mitzvot* of holy time, of Shabbat and other holidays.

WE CAN ADD TO THE HOLINESS OF TIME

The Jewish holidays have been described as resting places, like hotels or inns, at which our people meet as we journey through the year. On holidays, we set aside our daily concerns and come together to remember the sad times as well as the celebrations of our people. We remember God's presence in our history and the goodness of Creation. And we remember that God makes time holy and that we can add to time's holiness by observing the *mitzvot*.

> Which holidays are your favorites? Why? What *mitzvot*, such as lighting Ḥanukkah candles, hearing the *shofar*, and eating in a *sukkah*, can you perform to add to the holiness of time?

Guess Who's Coming to Dinner!

On Sukkot it's a tradition to perform the *mitzvah* of hospitality—*hachnasat orḥim*, "welcoming guests." We invite friends, neighbors, and relatives to the *sukkah*. It is also a custom to invite "special guests," called *ushpizin*. They are our biblical ancestors Abraham, Isaac, Jacob, Joseph, Moses, Aaron, and David. Name two other biblical heroes you would like to invite to your *sukkah*. Sarah? Isaiah? Ruth? Explain why you chose them.

Which modern righteous heroes might you want to invite? Are they famous people, such as Golda Meir and Jonas Salk? Or are they friends, teachers, or relatives? Explain your choices.

It's a Riddle

Here's a riddle: What has 12 branches, on every branch 4 twigs, and on each twig 7 leaves?
(The year! 12 months in a year, 4 weeks in a month, and 7 days in a week.)

Here's another riddle: What has letters that are never mailed, turns but is not round, and is not named for its bottom?
(A Ḥanukkah top—a *dreidel*)

Write two riddles or questions about Jewish holidays and share them with your classmates.

Let's Celebrate!

Draw a picture of or write about one of your favorite Jewish holidays.

We go through different stages in life. Each one has its own strengths. Older people have the experience and wisdom of their many years of living, while younger people have more energy and time to learn. What's special about being your age? What age do you look forward to being? Why?

Our tradition teaches that life is a gift from God and that God makes all life holy. How can you thank God for the gift of this year? How can you add to its holiness?

11

God Makes Living Holy

What are some of the events your family celebrates? Anniversaries? Birthdays? Graduations? Do you celebrate by having a party or eating special foods? Do you play music and exchange gifts? What else makes these events times to be remembered?

Just as we celebrate God's presence in Jewish history, so we celebrate God's presence in our lives.

MAKING MARRIAGE HOLY

The Bible describes the partnership, or Covenant, between the Jewish people and God as an everlasting marriage. God said to us: "I will betroth you forever. I will marry you with righteousness and justice, with loving-kindness and compassion."

What do these words from the Bible tell us about God's love for us? About how married couples can show their love for one another?

Our tradition teaches that couples add holiness to their lives when they marry. The Hebrew word for marriage, *kiddushin*, comes from the root of the Hebrew word for holy—*kadosh*.

The Jewish wedding ceremony includes a blessing that praises God for making us holy through the *mitzvah* of *kiddushin*. How do you think the performance of other holy acts, such as being kind, caring, and trustworthy, can remind a couple to welcome God's presence in their marriage?

The wedding ceremony also includes seven additional blessings, called the *sheva brachot*. These blessings ask God to grant peace and joy to the newlyweds and the Jewish people.

WELCOME TO THE *BRIT*!

When a Jewish child is born or adopted, we celebrate God's presence in that child's life. We also pray that the child will add to life's holiness by honoring our *Brit* with God.

A *Brit Milah* (Covenant of Circumcision) is performed on Jewish baby boys. When a Jewish girl is born, a *Simḥat Bat* (Celebration of a Daughter) ceremony is held. These rituals welcome children into the Jewish community and our Covenant with God. At these ceremonies, parents make the commitment to teach their children the *mitzvot* so they too can live as partners with God.

Why do you think our tradition teaches us to pray for the community when we celebrate our personal joys? Do you think this is an important tradition? Why or why not?

When a Jewish child is named and welcomed into the Covenant, blessings are recited, such as this: "May the parents raise their child filled with love of Torah and the desire to perform *mitzvot*, and may they be privileged to bring their child to the wedding canopy."

Babies are named at the *Brit Milah* and *Simhat Bat* ceremonies. Adam's baby sister received her name, Sarah, during Shabbat services in the synagogue. She has the same name as her great-great-grandmother. Many parents name their children after a relative who has died, hoping the person's good deeds will live on through their children's lives.

Were you named after someone? What do you know about that person?

**An ancient legend tells what our ancestors offered
in return for the gift of the Torah.**

For the Sake of the Children

Our sages tell us that when the Israelites stood at Mount Sinai, God said to them, "Before I give you My Torah, you must give me something that proves you will take good care of it."

The people thought long and hard about what to offer as proof of their love and devotion. They offered their jewelry—bracelets, rings, necklaces, and pins. But God refused to accept these as proof.

The Israelites thought some more about what was most precious to them. "Let us offer God the patriarchs—Abraham, Isaac, and Jacob—as proof of our good intentions," they said. But God refused them too.

Finally, the Israelites said, "Our children and all generations of children after them are what is most precious. We will teach them to love and obey God's commandments."

God was pleased. And God said, "For their sake, I will give you the Torah."

Our tradition teaches us that God gave the Torah for the sake of children and that God continues to protect the world because of the children who study Torah.

How does God's love and respect for you make you feel? How can you share that love and respect with others?

114

IN BLESSED MEMORY

The Jewish tradition includes the *mitzvah* of honoring the memory of people who have died. We honor the memory of family members when we say the *Kaddish* prayer.

Kaddish is recited at home during *shiva*, the first seven days of the mourning period. It is also recited as part of regular synagogue services.

Like the word *kiddushin*, *Kaddish* comes from the same root as the Hebrew word *kadosh*. When we recite *Kaddish*, we publicly praise God as we remember the many ways our loved one added holiness to life.

We also honor those we loved by contributing *tzedakah* in their memory, by naming children after them, by lighting a *yahrzeit* candle on the anniversary of their death, and by remembering their good deeds through our own. Each time we perform acts of loving-kindness and justice as they did, we keep their memory alive. In this way, their goodness lives on and continues to strengthen and guide us.

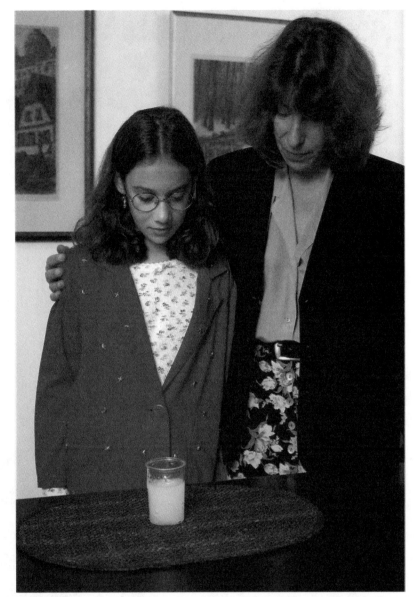

Each year, on the anniversary of a person's death, we light a *yahrzeit* candle at home and recite the *Kaddish* prayer in synagogue.

The *yahrzeit* candle reminds us that those who have died continue to light God's world through the *mitzvot* they performed. How can this knowledge encourage us to do our part to honor the Covenant?

BECOMING A FULL MEMBER OF THE COVENANT

After years of study, you will become a *bat* or *bar mitzvah*. That day will be one of great celebration, a joy for the entire community, for it will be the day you are welcomed as a full member of the *Brit*.

The ceremony for a *bar* or *bat mitzvah* celebrates a new beginning—the start of more serious learning, and acceptance of additional responsibilities and honors.

For example, as a *bat* or *bar mitzvah* you may be counted as a member of a *minyan*, a prayer group which requires at least ten Jewish adults. You may receive an *aliyah*, the honor of reciting the blessings before and after verses from a Torah portion are chanted. And you may fulfill the *mitzvah* of wearing a prayer shawl, or *tallit*, and putting on *tefillin*.

While it is a *mitzvah* to celebrate becoming a *bat* or *bar mitzvah*, remember that it is also a *mitzvah* to share a portion of your gifts with the needy. Giving *tzedakah* will add even more holiness to this great day.

Once you become a *bar* or *bat mitzvah*, you will remain one all your life. How will you continue to honor our Covenant with God as you grow older and more mature?

Your partnership with God and the Jewish community is just beginning. Through each blessing, ceremony, and act of remembrance in which you participate, you will add to the holiness of life.

Some adults did not have the opportunity to study when they were young. By beginning their Jewish studies as adults, they follow in the tradition of Rabbi Akiba, who didn't learn the letters of the Hebrew alphabet until he was 40.

When to Say What

When we mark events in a lifetime, there are prayers we recite. Read the three below and connect each one to the life-cycle event at which it is said.

Praised are You, Adonai, who causes the groom to rejoice with his bride.

בָּרוּךְ אַתָּה, ה',

מְשַׂמֵּחַ חָתָן עִם הַכַּלָּה.

As he entered the Covenant, so too may he enter a life of Torah, marriage, and good deeds.

כְּשֵׁם שֶׁנִּכְנַס לַבְּרִית,

כֵּן יִכָּנֵס לְתוֹרָה וּלְחֻפָּה

וּלְמַעֲשִׂים טוֹבִים.

Praised are You, Adonai, who gives the Torah.

בָּרוּךְ אַתָּה, ה',

נוֹתֵן הַתּוֹרָה.

My Name

Jews believe that certain qualities—intelligence, humor, thoughtfulness—can come like a blessing with a name. Jewish families from Europe and Russia usually name a child after a relative who has died. Jews from Spain and the Middle East often name children after living relatives. When we name a child after someone, we hope the child will develop the qualities or characteristics of the person who originally had the name.

I WAS NAMED AFTER:

COMPLETE NAME (English): _____

COMPLETE NAME (Hebrew): _____

FAMILY RELATIONSHIP TO ME: _____

Find out as much as you can about the person after whom you were named and record the information here:

_____

_____

_____

_____

What three *mitzvot* can you fulfill to honor this person?

_____

_____

_____

Exploring new places can be fun, but not when you're lost. Have you ever lost your way while taking a walk or riding a bike? Were the road signs confusing? Did you wish you had a map or compass? What did you do?

12

Partners in the Covenant

The Jewish people are sometimes described as "wanderers." We wandered through the Sinai wilderness for 40 years and, for centuries after the destruction of the Second Temple, we wandered throughout the world searching for a place to live according to God's laws.

But though we wandered, we were not lost. To this day, we are guided by our spiritual map, the Torah. And when we stray, God's presence is like a compass that points us in the right direction.

CONTINUING THE JOURNEY

Each generation since the Exodus has done its part to honor the *Brit* and add holiness to the world through the *mitzvot*. Each generation has added its wisdom while passing on our tradition. You are now the inheritor of this tradition with its dream of a complete and perfect world. Now it is your turn.

God and Torah are the compass and map that will guide you on your journey. And each *mitzvah* you fulfill will be a marker on the way to a better world.

Your family, teachers, friends, and the members of your synagogue are among the many people of *klal Yisrael*, the Jewish community, who will be part of your journey. They will work and pray with you, celebrate with you, and comfort you when you're sad. When problems or disagreements arise, it is with them that you will learn to set aside conflict so that solutions can be found. And it is your faith in God that will help you succeed.

Michael and his grandfather are on a camping trip. There are many paths from which they must choose. Sometimes, it's difficult to figure out which one is the right one. So, they use a map and compass to guide them.

How can Torah guide you like a map when you need to make choices? How can your awareness of God's presence point you in the right direction?

Fortunately people are not machine-made like pennies or dollar bills. Each of us is unique. Every one of us is an original!

What do you think the world would be like if everyone had the same interests and abilities? If everyone wanted to play soccer, who would be on the baseball team? If everyone was a doctor, who would make movies or build cars? If you didn't understand a math problem, who could help you if everyone was the same?

EVERY PERSON IS IMPORTANT

Our sages taught that God makes every person different. Each of us is "one of a kind." This means that no one exactly like you ever lived before. So you can be sure that God created you for a special purpose, a purpose no one else ever had.

That is why every Jew has an important part in honoring the *Brit*. Each of us can contribute something unique, something only we can give. And when we make our contributions, we add holiness to God's world.

What contributions do you make? Do you call or visit friends or relatives who are ill? Participate in synagogue services? Give money to *tzedakah* and speak respectfully to others?

What other *mitzvot* do you fulfill to help complete Creation?

This first attempt to bake a cake hasn't gone very well at all. Perhaps these boys will do better next time, or maybe they'll never be successful bakers. We're all part of God's Creation and each of us has a unique and special contribution to make. But it's not always easy to discover what our contribution might be. So we try many things and work with many people to discover what our strengths and weaknesses are.

Even when we fail, it is our responsibility to keep on trying. For as Rabbi Tarfon taught us, none of us has to complete the world, but each of us must do our part.

LET THERE BE LIGHT

Our tradition teaches that just as each person has a contribution to make, so has each nation. The purpose of the Jewish people is to live as partners with God by honoring the *Brit*.

We try our best to work as one community, bringing our strengths together to make the world a better place. Often we are successful, but sometimes—because we're human— we fail.

Sometimes we fail because we have difficulty cooperating with others. Sometimes it's because we need to learn from our mistakes or work a little harder. And sometimes we fail because there isn't anything more we can do. The solutions to some problems aren't in our control, they're in God's hands.

When we work and pray together we learn to do our part. And that is all we are asked to do.

Just as God brought light into the world on the first day of Creation, so it is our task to continually add light by performing God's *mitzvot*. May your life be long and the light you add be bright and everlasting. May each *mitzvah* you fulfill contribute to the holiness of the Jewish people and to the glory of God's name.

Let us go now. The hour is late and there is much to be done. *Lech l'cha*, "Go forward," for you shall be a blessing and you shall be blessed.

Your Contributions to Making Our Dream Come True

The purpose of the Jewish people is to make the dream of a better world come true.

How can you improve your life by honoring our Covenant with God?

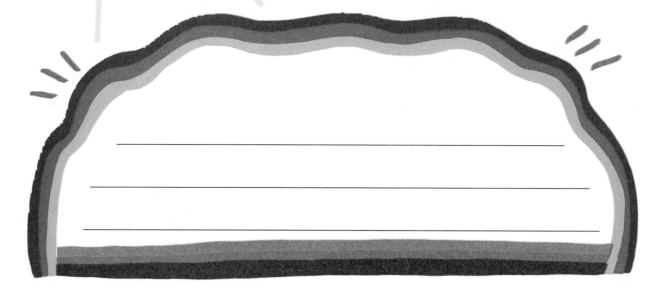

How can you contribute to peace and goodness in your family's life by honoring our Covenant with God?

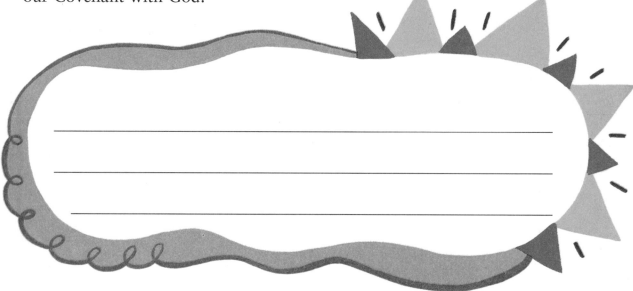